Lions in Our Garden:

A Biographical Report of the Adventures and Thrilling Life of Pamela Goodman

by

Pamela Goodman

DORRANCE
PUBLISHING CO
EST. 1920
PITTSBURGH, PENNSYLVANIA 15238

The contents of this work, including, but not limited to, the accuracy of events, people, and places depicted; opinions expressed; permission to use previously published materials included; and any advice given or actions advocated are solely the responsibility of the author, who assumes all liability for said work and indemnifies the publisher against any claims stemming from publication of the work.

All Rights Reserved
Copyright © 2022 by Pamela Goodman

No part of this book may be reproduced or transmitted, downloaded, distributed, reverse engineered, or stored in or introduced into any information storage and retrieval system, in any form or by any means, including photocopying and recording, whether electronic or mechanical, now known or hereinafter invented without permission in writing from the publisher.

Dorrance Publishing Co
585 Alpha Drive
Suite 103
Pittsburgh, PA 15238
Visit our website at *www.dorrancebookstore.com*

ISBN: 978-1-6393-7038-2
eISBN: 978-1-6393-7827-2

Dedicated to my friend, Claire Messier
for all her help with my first book.

Also to my children and grandchildren.

CHAPTER 1

Our Parents and Early Childhood

My father was born in Potchefstrom near Johannesburg, the capital of South Africa. When he was in his late teens, his father committed suicide. He shot himself at the local swimming pool. No one ever mentioned the reason for this tragedy.

He left a widow and five children, and since my father was the eldest, he ended his education and worked to help support the family. Much later two of his sisters moved to Nairobi, capital of Kenya, East Africa, where they both gained employment. Elsie, the older sister, met and married an Englishman, and they purchased a beautiful farm in Nanyuki situated on the slopes of Mount Kenya. There was a trout stream running through the farm. Their pet cat used to occasionally scoop out a fish with her paw and enjoy a delicious meal!

Peggy, Dad's younger sister, married a successful businessman from the United Kingdom. He was known as "Martini" (W. H. Martin). He was well known in Nairobi, especially at the "Long Bar" in the New Stanley Hotel. He owned a talkative pet parrot who could perfectly imitate the sound of the soda siphon Martini used to calm his whiskey in the evening at "sundowner" time.

He built a beautiful home, South African Cape style, for Peggy and their two daughters. Since his remaining siblings were now employed adults, my dad decided also to move to East Africa. He rode his motorcycle thousands of miles from South to East Africa, mostly on dirt roads. There may have been the danger of wild animals along the roads. I wish I had learned more details of his perilous journey.

My dad was a good-looking guy with brown hair and hazel eyes, plus a killer smile. He was an honest, hardworking man, very well liked by the Europeans and Africans. My brother and I both loved and respected him. Our dad was of Dutch and French heritage. His name was Eric Arnold Jansen, but everyone called him "Jan."

My mother was born in Surrey, England. She was a dancer at the famous London Palladium, a member of the "Fisher Girls" troupe. Her name was Dorothy Sinclair (aka Dolly). She danced in a show starring the famous comedian Tommy Handley. This was the era of the "Roaring Twenties." The Fisher Girls toured all over the U.K. and danced in Paris. My mum was offered the position of dance teacher there, but she was too busy enjoying touring with the troupe. She and two other dancers took the train to Nice in the South of France to dance in a movie starring Fernand Grave and Betty Balfour. She was a petite brunette, very attractive and with lots of personality. During her dancing days at the Palladium, she met and later became engaged to Tony Ramsden, the Earl of Ramsden's nephew. He was a regular "Stage Door Johnny." They were the men who used to hang around the stage door hoping to meet the stars and dancers.

He took her to the family estate to meet future relatives. In the evening a party was held to celebrate their engagement. Lady Ramsden lent Mum a beautiful gown to wear. In the wee small hours Mum was teaching the guests how to dance the Charleston, a dance popular in the Roaring Twenties.

Before their marriage, Tony invited Mum and her mother (as chaperone) to take a cruise to East Africa. They docked in Mumbasa, Kenya, on the Indian Ocean. They visited the beautiful island of Zanzibar. It was mostly populated by Arabs and a few East Indians. They were invited to the sultan's palace. They sat around with him on floor pillows while he smoked his hookah pipe. Unfortunately for him, Mum discovered that Tony was keeping a mistress on the island. He had the means to visit her occasionally and had no intention of breaking off the relationship. She broke off her engagement to him and asked him to take her mother back to England, as she had decided to stay in Africa.

Tony sailed away, out of her life, taking her mother back home as my mother was feeling the blow of being jilted.

Mother moved to Daresalaam, capital of Tanganyika, also situated on the shores of the Indian Ocean. Eric Jansen arrived and made a reservation at the same hotel. They met there and eventually married, later moving to Mombasa on the coast of Kenya. My dad landed a job with the Shell Oil Company. My brother, Michael William, was born there. Everyone called him Mike. The company put on a lovely big party and dance at the local club for the employees. Everyone was dining, drinking, and dancing. Dad asked the boss's wife to dance, thinking it would be the "right thing" to do. Unfortunately, Mum, who'd had one too many brandies, found Dad and his partner on the dance floor, and in a jealous rage, she removed her shoe and proceeded to hit the boss's wife. Thankfully no serious damage was done, but needless to say, it was the end of Dad's career with the Shell Oil Company!

When Mike was about three years old, they moved up country to the goldfields in Kakamega, Kenya, where Dad was hoping to strike gold. Mum was pregnant again, and I was born in a makeshift hospital, in an older house situated on the mine. The day I came into the world, Dad went off to the local pub to celebrate with some of his pals before visiting us. By this time he was feeling no pain, and as he was leaving the hospital, he fell down a few steps into the garden below and promptly fell asleep. The day nurse found him there in the morning, still asleep among the flowers!

We got used to the adults' heavy drinking. Since we no longer had an "Ayah" (nursemaid) whilst they were partying in clubs and hotels, we would fall asleep in the car. There were many loud and frightening rows once we arrived home. This was partly due to the alcohol consumed, but it was mostly because of Mum's extreme bouts of jealousy.

CHAPTER 2

Not much gold was discovered in Kakamega, so now we moved to Geita in Tanganyika. This time we were at a big gold mine owned by some Canadian businessmen. There were about fifty European employees and almost one hundred Africans. Dad was the labor manager in charge of the African workforce. By this time he spoke fluent Swahili. The Africans seemed to like and respect him.

We had a nice house with five servants. It was situated across from the local clubhouse, so our parents used to walk over there to meet up with friends, play roulette, drink, party, and sometimes watch old movies. Every evening before dinner we'd sit on the verandah to watch the beautiful crimson and purple sunsets. Our parents would indulge in their evening sundowners. Mike and I would sip on cream sodas. When I was four, so I'm told, I passed out by the front steps. Dad picked me up and carried me in his arms across the street to the small mine hospital. My temperature was sky high. The resident East Indian doctor laid me in a bathtub filled with ice. All our neighbors were bringing their ice cube trays to the hospital. I finally regained consciousness, and my temperature receded to almost normal. The doctor's diagnosis was cerebral malaria. He saved my life. Thank you, Dr. Patel. In a few days I was up and home and running all over the place.

There was the addition of life in the form of a new pet, a young vervet monkey with grey fur, and a black face, hands, and feet. A "toto Kidogo" (small boy) was selling him. He told us the monkey was an orphan. I begged Mom and Dad. They finally gave in and gave the toto a few schillings. We named the monkey Jacko. He slept in a box by my bed. He loved peanuts and bananas. Dad built him his own house, a box on a tall wooden pole, so he was safe. He stayed close to home mostly. When he ventured out, he'd usually get into some mischief.

Jacko

East Africa

Our next-door neighbor was a gentleman from Belgium. Every morning he'd pop his bread in the toaster then wander off to shave or whatever. As soon as Jacko heard the toast pop up, he'd jump through the window and grab it. We'd hear Mr. Carbonell yelling. Uh oh! Jacko's stolen his toast again.

The neighbors who lived behind us were an interesting couple. He was from Czechoslovakia, she was Austrian, but word was out that she was a Nazi sympathizer. They had a pet cheetah who used to sit on a barstool in their living room. He would regard guests with disdain. We were all used to people having exotic pets. Lion cubs, iguanas, monkeys, of course, and our friend Mona had a mongoose with his own swimming pool.

Now the Austrian lady, being a Nazi sympathizer, was not too popular with the British contingent, as you can imagine. It was during the war, of course, circa 1942. She was a sour-faced person. She wore a rather tatty hair piece. When at home, she tended to leave it in her bedroom on the dressing table. Well, one morning when Jacko was out exploring, he saw her bedroom window was open. He decided to have a look around since she was out of the room. Lo and behold, he saw a piece of "fur" or maybe a dead mouse on her dresser. He grabbed it and ran home to climb a tall free.

We were having a relaxed breakfast when we heard loud screaming and cursing in German. We ran out to see what was going on. There was Elsa at the base of the tree in a state of great excitement and rage, and there was Jacko, high up in the tree, dangling her hairpiece enticingly. We were bent double trying to stifle our laughter. Finally, I had to climb halfway up the tree with a peeled banana to try and coax Jacko down. Of course, when he saw the banana, he promptly dropped the hairpiece and clambered down to claim his reward.

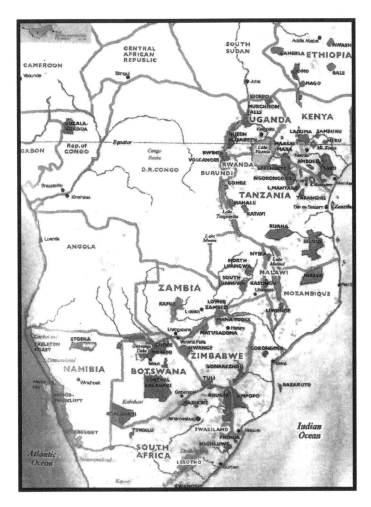

One night, when my parents were across the street, somehow safari fire ants got into my bed. The stinging from the ants woke me. So painful! I started screaming. Our faithful African night watchman heard me. He ran across to the clubhouse to tell my dad something was terribly wrong. Dad came rushing home, took my nightie off, and started pulling the stingers out. He put soothing lotion all over my body and burnt my nightgown. The pain stayed for two days, and I had red welts all over my body.

One very early morning, about three o'clock, our parents came home to wake us up. Dad said, "Hurry up, we're going crocodile bashing!" There were two or three carloads of very tipsy friends, everyone heading out to the lake. Once there, we all climbed into the African canoes, which were not being used at night. We used the paddles to tap the crocs when we saw those two bumps of their eyes showing just above the water. It was all very exciting. Everyone was laughing loudly. Some of the men were actually standing up in the canoes. It was a miracle that no one fell in considering they'd all had a lot to drink. They may have been gobbled up!

By this time Mike was eight and I was five. Mum decided to teach us by correspondence course. She had taught us to read already. She persevered for a while but soon off-loaded us onto another mine lady who was teaching a few of the local kids. By the time Mike was ten, he was sent off to boarding school in Nakuru, Kenya. It was a boys only school.

When I was seven, I was sent to a co-ed school, Greensteads. It had been a farm several miles from Nakuru. There were no schools in Tanganyika at the time, so we had a long journey to school in Kenya. There were several other kids on the lake steamer, so we made some new friends. We sailed on Lake Victoria from Mwanza, two nights on the boat, then docked in Kisuma, Kenya. Aboard, we were on the lower deck. One day I was standing at the foot of the stairs leading to the first class upper deck. I saw a vision of loveliness coming down the stairs; it was Rita Hayworth! She was gorgeous. She had long, wavy red hair, a floaty chiffon dress, and a picture hat. She was closely followed by Ali Khan, to whom she was married at the time. I was thrilled to see her so close. She was a big Hollywood star in those days. She and Ali Kahn were married in 1949. They had a daughter, Princess Yasmin, but divorced in 1953. He offered Rita one million dollars if she would raise Yasmin as a Muslim, but she refused and told him Yasmin was going to grow up in America in freedom as a Christian.

The Aga Kahn was Persian, Ali Kahn's father. He had thousands of Muslim followers in Kenya. Once we docked in Kisumu after two nights aboard the steamer, we then boarded the train to Nakuru where our schools were located. From the station, we were bussed to our separate schools. The train was an overnight ride. It was a wonderful experience. We saw so many animals along the way: zebra, wildebeests, dik-diks, and sometimes even a lion or two.

At Greensteads School the girls slept in dormitories consisting of maybe twelve beds. We each had our own lockers for gym clothes and personal items. The classrooms held a mixture of boys and girls. There was a French boy who sat behind me. He'd throw wads of paper at me to get my attention. I turned around and he had his penis exposed. I couldn't stand him. He wrote me notes saying he'd like to fuck with me. I was seven years old and didn't have a clue what fuck meant. I shoved his notes in my locker.

I did have a boyfriend. He was kind of nerdy and wore glasses, but he'd come to my rescue if I was being bullied. He made a soapstone heart for me and painted our initials on it. I put that in my locker too. A few days later, when we were all in the dining room eating lunch, the headmistress walked in carrying the drawer from a locker. I was summoned to her office. It was my drawer!! She held up the French boy's notes and the soapstone heart. I tried to explain that I didn't understand what was the meaning of the notes. She ignored me and explained I was to be expelled. I was not to attend any more classes and to pack my belongings. My parents would be notified that I would be returning home ASAP. So now I had to make the long journey home alone. In fact, it was her daughter who should have been expelled. She used to visit the boy's dormitory late at night. She knew that I knew, but I never did report her.

Mum and Dad took us to a "professional" Indian photographer (note the dead flowers). Mike was ten, Pam seven.

CHAPTER 3

Now mother decided I should attend the convent just outside Nairobi, the capital of Kenya. This was mainly a Catholic school. I was Protestant. It was a great expense for my dad. So I was shunted off to the convent. When I was thirteen, one night on the lake steamer I noticed blood on my pajamas. I was terrified. Luckily one of the older girls aboard could explain that I had started my period and supplied the necessary equipment. My mother had never discussed this issue with me and, in fact, had called me a little whore when I was only eleven years old. She was very verbally and physically abusive at times. I can only think she was jealous of my close relationship with my father.

My brother was now attending The Prince of Wales boy's school across from the convent. He was only allowed to visit me once a month whereas the boys from St. Mary's Catholic School could visit their convent sisters every Sunday. Some of the nuns were quite mean-spirited. I was talking to a friend at lunch with my elbow resting on the marble tabletop. A nun crept up behind me and bashed my elbow on that hard surface several times! Another time a nun, Mother Peter Claver, was giving an algebra lesson. It was difficult for all of us. After class I told her I was having a problem with one of the questions. She refused to help, saying, "You won't understand, you're a Protestant!"

Mother Hyacinth and Mother Phillippa were the nicest, kindest nuns. Mother Superior drank a lot of the chapel wine. She was always falling and injuring herself. During the Catholic Ritual of Corpus Christie, we were allowed out of bounds to gather wildflowers. We would then scatter them along the avenue between St. Mary's Boy's School and our convent, a distance of about two hundred yards.

On the appointed day, the Catholic fathers would trample over all our flowers singing hymns, swaying incense, and praying. Since we were allowed off the school grounds on that one day, my brother (whose school was just across the street from ours) wrote to Mother Superior telling her that his school was having a fete that day and asking permission for me and a few friends to attend the fete for a short time. She never responded.

We decided to go anyway, the five of us. My brother met us and bought us all a Coke. We went through "The Chamber of Horrors." After that we panicked and decided to dash back to the convent. There were three nuns waiting to tell us we were all to be expelled. We couldn't believe it. We were only gone about twenty minutes. Everyone else was out of bounds picking wildflowers. We were not allowed in class. We all had to stay in one room until our parents could find a way to get us home. My brother wrote again to Mother Superior begging her to reconsider. My Catholic Uncle Martini, who lived in Nairobi, paid her a visit. His two daughters were day boarders at the convent. She was unbending in her decision.

So now we five girls were confined to one large room, alone, forbidden to mingle with other friends. We were all Protestants. It may have been a different outcome if we were of the Catholic faith. We played cards all day and teased one another whilst we waited for transportation to various areas of East Africa. The nuns told us we should be praying for our sins.

SINNERS

LORETO CONVENT 1949 THE DAY OF EXPULSION
NAIROBI KENYA

CHAPTER 4

I was so miserable and couldn't wait for Mike to come home for the holidays. By this time we had moved to Mwanza, still in Tanganyika, located on the shores of Lake Victoria, a small town with wide, sandy streets lined with picturesque Jakaranda trees. Dad had an office in town. He now worked for the Sisal Labor Bureau.

Our house was just a few miles from town. Mother had her own bedroom. Dad and I shared the second bedroom, a strange arrangement, and Mike slept in a makeshift room off the dining room. At night I could hear the hyenas making strange laughing noises. Sometimes they would come in our garden. I could hear them crunching on bones. I was terrified of them.

After an age, Mike came home. I was so glad to see him. There was a huge mango tree in our back garden laden with mangos. We'd have them for breakfast – delicious. Mum would take her nap in the afternoon. Mike and I would play with Jacko outside. One afternoon four or five African children climbed the tree and stuffed mangos in their shirts and pockets; we were out of sight, so they felt safe. For some reason, Mum woke up from her nap. She quietly came out the back door. She had a shotgun. When she saw the *totos* in the tree, she fired a shot in the air! The *totos* fell out of the tree, "like ripe mangos," she said, laughing her head off. The *totos* ran away and never came back.

Dad had a nice office, behind which was a rocky hill. When Mike came home we often visited Dad at work. A large group of monkeys lived up on the rocky hill. Mike decided we should try to catch one as a playmate for Jacko. We clambered up the hill with a few yards of thick twine and some bananas. Mike made a lasso loop of the twine and placed it on a large, flat rock with a half-peeled banana in the center. After a few minutes along came a baby monkey. He grabbed the banana. Mike pulled the string so the loop closed over his wrist. We had him!!

Now came the big daddy monkeys, yelling and baring their teeth at us. We quickly released the baby then made a hasty retreat back down to Dad's office. We were scared out of our wits but so relieved to be safe.

Another bright idea of Mike's was to take apart the leftover Christmas crackers and remove the banger strips. We then tied them together to form an eight-foot length. We strung them about twelve inches high across the path next to our house. This was the route taken by some of the African women (*bibis*) every evening on their way home after partying in various bars after work.

We hid in the bushes to await the "ambush." Eventually they came giggling and staggering all over the place. Then their legs hit our string – BANG, BANG, BANG – they leapt in the air screaming and shouting. We were in hysterics hidden in the bushes. I set up a stand beside the path. I found a few empty bottles, washed them, then filled them with water and red food coloring. I then added a few drops of Dad's scented hair oil. I arranged them on my stand and sold them as perfume. I kept the prices low – ten or fifteen cents per bottle. The African ladies were good customers. I sold them all and made about two shillings. I was very proud of myself. Then Mike told me they only purchased my perfume because they wanted the bottles. My joy was deflated - even more so when I was reprimanded by Dad for using some of his hair oil.

Mum decided now that I should attend another convent, this one situated in Eldoret. Thank goodness Dad refused, as he could no longer afford the high fees. Thus, my education ended when I was fourteen.

At sundowner time, early evening in Mwanza, we'd all sit on the verandah sipping our drinks and munching on *zamoozas*, waiting for the always-glorious sunset. Dad would bring out three dining chairs and set them in a row facing the house. We'd stand on the chairs holding badminton racquets. Bats would come flying out of the roof for their evening prowl. We'd try to swat them down with our racquets. That was our evening's entertainment. We hated those bats, the stench of them, and their everlasting squealing.

We were with our parents at the local hotel one evening when Mr. Mavricos, the Greek gentleman who owned the hotel, invited everyone aboard his boat anchored at the dock of Lake Victoria. He wanted to take us all sailing. Mike and I were pretty excited. A good idea, someone suggested, would be to travel across to Nungwe. Everyone thought that a great idea, including Mr. George Mavricos. Provisions, mainly alcoholic, were loaded on board. The passengers boarded. The party raged on and George shouted down the voice tube to the engine room, where the crew had started the engine and were awaiting further instructions. "Full speed ahead, hand to starboard," he instructed, and no one gave it another thought.

Late the following morning one of the guests groggily raised himself on one elbow and peered through the porthole; the engines were still revving, the propellers thrashing the water, but the vessel was still tied to the Mwanza jetty. The crew had been awaiting the instruction from George to cast off from the jetty! So we never even moved.

Dad once took me to an *ngoma* (a daytime tribal celebration involving the beating of drums, singing, and dancing). Only the men participated. Their faces were painted. They were bare-chested but wore palm leaf skirts over their shorts, and their necks were adorned with ceremonial beads. A huge crowd of Africans formed a circle around the participants. Men, women, and a few children made up the audience. Dad and I were the only Europeans present. I was only seven, still quite small, so I couldn't see the tribal dancers. A group of Africans kindly stood aside so Dad could guide me to a better view. One of the celebrants was dancing with a huge snake wound around his neck. He danced over to me and held the snake's face close to mine. I was scared, but Dad held tightly onto my shoulders and laughed at the performer – he knew it was harmless.

One day Mike and I were hiking in a rather unknown area. It was quite deserted with no sign of any African huts. We were looking for a dry riverbed. All of a sudden a huge python, at least six feet long, slithered across the path a few feet in front of us. We froze without even a whisper or any movement. He kept going, thanks be to God. He disappeared into the bush. WHEW!

Another time our houseboy, Ndongo, called out to Dad, "*Kuja pesi Bwana!*" (Come quickly, sir), bring your gun!" There was a big puff adder in his house. He was nudging it with his foot as if it was a play thing! This is probably the most poisonous snake in Africa. Dad had to shoot it very quickly.

Mike and I did eventually find the dry riverbed. There were tall trees on both sides with long, thick vines hanging down, maybe ten feet long. We called them "monkey ropes." Mike showed me how to hold onto the end of one and swing across the river. I was scared, but he said, "Come on, Titch!" This was his nickname for me. "Don't be a scaredy-cat." He gave me a shove, and I was flying across a very wide river to the other side. I loved it. I felt like a bird flying. We stayed there two or three hours. We often returned.

Whilst still in Mwanza there was yet another social evening at the hotel. We kids were allowed to join in as it was still early evening. There was a new addition to the usual group; he was tall with dark hair and a beard. He said he could play guitar. It was in his room in the hotel annex. He asked me to go and fetch it and gave me his room key. I was looking forward to hearing him play, so I ran over to the annex and found his room, but the key wouldn't work. I tried and tried. Was about to give up when he came along and managed to get the door open. He led me inside. I was excited to hear him play. Unfortunately, he had other plans. Now I was only eleven, but I was beginning to feel uneasy. He started groping me, then shoved his hand up my panties. I was really scared now. I tried to push him away but he was a big, strong guy. Somehow I managed to break away from him and ran back to the hotel.

I asked Mum to come with me to the ladies room, but once we arrived, I wasn't able to tell what he'd tried to do to me. She kept asking, "What is wrong?" I was too afraid and ashamed to tell her. I said I was tired, so she took me to the car and laid me down in the back seat. All my later life I felt that men with beards were rather repulsive.

Another evening at the hotel my parents met up with a rich American, Tom Kennedy. He asked Dad to take him duck shooting. Dad agreed to meet him the next day. Mike and I and our spaniel dog, Sally, were allowed to tag along. It was early morning when we arrived at a big, swampy area. The men and my brother forged ahead, Sally and I bringing up the rear. In some places the swampy water was quite deep. Sally and I had to "dog paddle" part of the way. The men bagged a few ducks. Kennedy was very pleased. The next day he took Mike and me shopping. He bought us each a brand new bicycle! We were thrilled.

One evening we took our sundowners to the beach next to the cemetery. It was peaceful and cool there. Dad rented a small canoe so Mike and I could paddle across the lake. We were so enjoying ourselves when all of a sudden we felt a big bump. We looked down, and it was a large hippo! We paddled furiously back to shore. If the hippo had tipped us out, he may have bitten large chunks from us or a croc would have found us to be a tasty meal. The African women used to wash clothes in the lake. A couple were pulled under and taken by the crocs.

One day near the cemetery, we saw a huge croc basking in the sun on a large rock near the lakeshore. Mike decided to take a shot at it with his .22 rifle. He hit the croc in his eye and he died!! We couldn't believe it. A shot in a million! Several Africans appeared out of nowhere and dragged the croc's body to shore. Mike was now a hero! A photographer came to take photos of him holding his rifle with one foot on the croc's body. Photos were sent to Remington Rand who sent him boxes of free ammo. It was written up in the *East African Standard*.

Now Mum decided we should move again, this time to Kenya. There was a Sisal farm for lease in Kitale, about two hundred miles from Nairobi. She talked Dad into it. He didn't have much choice. She was in command. We loved Mwanza and were very sad to leave. Off we went again, my fourth move since I was born.

Travel East Africa Style

CHAPTER 5

Kitale

The farm was about fifteen miles from the small town of Kitale. There was a sports club where Mike belonged to a rugby team. Mum and Dad used to take me to watch his games, to have sundowners afterwards in the clubhouse, and to sometimes dance and watch movies. Mike was eighteen now. He'd graduated from the Prince of Wales and earned his high school certificate. He helped Dad a lot on the farm, driving the tractor and making fire breaks. During the dry season we experienced several fires.

We were responsible for collecting the eggs, washing them, and stamping them with K.F.A. (Kenya Farmers Association). We hated the egg collecting; the eggs would be covered in chicken poo. Mum kept turkeys and ducks as well as the chickens.

We had several "exotic" pets. The monkey, of course, and a Maribou stork with a huge, long beak. We also had a wild hare that used to sleep on Mum's feet when she was sitting down near the fireplace. There were also cats and dogs. One day our houseboy ran in to tell Mum the Maribou stork was eating her turkey chicks! We all ran out to see him tossing the chicks in the air, catching them in his wide-open beak, and swallowing them whole! That put an end to his stay with us. Dad put him in the car and took him for a long, one-way drive into the bush. Hopefully he would find some of his own kin there.

By this time I desperately needed to get away from my mother's constant verbal and physical abuse. If Dad was particularly attentive towards me or if he and I were just joking around, she would find a reason to abuse me. I would run to my room crying. Dad would come later and slip a note under the door, telling me how sorry he felt for me and somewhat ashamed that he hadn't tried to stop Mum's abuse. We both knew there would have been fireworks if he had intervened.

We used to light a fire in the evenings after it cooled off. Kitale was in the highlands, some six thousand feet above sea level.

Our neighbors on one side were Flora and Barney Mackie. Flora decided to open a day camp for children around the ages of ten to twelve. She had a large house, enough room for games and romping about. She asked my parents if I could come every day to help entertain the children. My parents agreed, and Dad would drive me over each morning. There were five children. I used to take them on hikes, home for lunch, then games and art lessons in the afternoons. The parents would collect them about five o'clock. Flora was a very heavy drinker. She was a big woman with fiery red hair, whereas Barney was quite short and somewhat intimidated by her. She was annoyed with Barney one afternoon. She started shouting and pulled out a revolver. She started taking potshots at him. I got the kids to hide down low behind the couch. Lucky for everyone she was a lousy shot, so she missed injuring everybody. I quickly called all the parents to tell them what had happened. They came immediately to take the children home.

That was a short-lived career for me; I don't remember if I was ever even paid! Weeks later my dad purchased a small, square car with spoke wheels for me. I had obtained employment in a dental office in town. The dentist was Doctor Walmsley. He actually lived in Eldoret, about fifty miles from Kitale. He only came in two days a week. I was alone in the office most of the time. I kept the place clean, answered the phone, and made his appointments. He showed me how to mend false teeth. When he had extractions to perform, he had me stand by holding a white plate for him to drop the bloody, smelly teeth on.

Driving home one evening in my little square convertible, the canvas top unfurled and blew over my face! I couldn't see, of course, and ended up in a ditch. I managed to untangle myself from the canvas but there was no way I could push the car out of the ditch! All of a sudden three young Africans appeared, laughing and joking at my predicament. Then they simply lifted my car out of the ditch in about five minutes. They refused to accept any "*baksheesh*" (tip money). They were so good like that. Always ready to help.

The family used to take walks in the evening; leading the walk was Sally, our spaniel, with Jacko riding on her back. Sometimes the Maribou stork would join us.

Mike had left for the big city - Nairobi, capital of Kenya. He landed a good job with Massey Ferguson, the tractor builders. Meanwhile the local preacher, Reverend Boxley and his wife, offered me a paid position caring for their three small children, as the parents were absent most of the day. I had a small bedroom at the back of the house and a tiny bathroom with a sink and toilet only. I had to shower in the main house.

I enjoyed the children; we played games in the mornings and I read to them. After lunch they took short naps. Later I would take them for short walks. The parents would usually be home for dinner. Later the reverend and I would drive over to the clubhouse to play badminton with the famous Louis Leakey, archaeologist. He and his wife, Mary, established an excavation site at Olduvai Gorge to search for fossils whose discoveries proved that human beings were far older than previously stated. It was said that Louis Leakey was the archaeologist who discovered the remains of "Lucy," said to be one of the first humans in Africa.

One German professor found a Homo sapiens skeleton in 1913 in Tanganyika (now Tanzania), and a professor in South Africa found a child's skull there in 1924. But archaeologists denied that these bones were significant. The first to make credible finds were this English couple, Louis and Mary Leakey.

Pamela Goodman

Louis Leakey
Archaeologist

Louis Seymour Bazett Leakey, also known as L
Kenyan paleoanthropologist and archaeologist \
important in demonstrating that humans evolved
Wikipedia

Born: August 7, 1903, Kabete, Kenya
Died: October 1, 1972, London, United Kingdor
Education: University of Cambridge
Spouse: Mary Leakey (m. 1936–1972), Henriet
1928–1936)
Siblings: Julia Barham, Douglas Leakey, Glad

Books

The Stone   Mau Mau   Unveiling   D
Age   and the   man's   N
Cultures... Kikuyu   origins   1!
1931   1952   1969

Lucy and the Leakeys' (article) Khan Academy https://www.khanacademy-org/partner-content/big-history.../lucy-and-the-leakeys

I had been seeing, on a platonic basis (so far), a good looking Australian rugby player, Alistair — tall, well-built with untidy dark blonde hair and lovely smiling blue eyes. I was off on the weekends so he drove me to Eldoret where he was playing in a rugby game. There was to be a dance later, so I watched the game, then he showered and changed. We joined in the dancing. We had a lovely evening and much later he introduced me to his friend, Walter. Since Alistair had another rugby game the following day, he asked Walter to give me a lift home as I had to attend to the children the next day. I wasn't too thrilled about this arrangement. Walter had a lot to drink and I didn't like the

26

look of him — very tall, black hair, thick red lips, bristly black mustache. I didn't have much choice. We piled into his big truck.

After he'd driven a half hour or so, he asked me to take over!! I had never driven a big truck and told him so. He said he was very tired (and drunk). I did manage to drive a few miles. Then Walter took over again. I was very tired so he suggested I should lie down in the back of the truck where there was a blanket I could lie on. I did fall asleep but started to wake up when the truck stopped. Walter climbed into the back, I thought to wake me up. Oh no! Next thing I knew he was laying on top of me, pulling up my skirt. I tried to push him off, but he was so big. I should have screamed but didn't want the reverend to witness what was happening or to wake the children. Instead I had to give in to rape by this revolting man. "Oh my God," he said when he saw that I was bleeding profusely. He'd taken away my virginity – at age fifteen. I ran into the house, into my small bathroom to wash myself, to wash him away! I threw away the clothes I was wearing. I never told anyone of the horrible sexual abuse I had suffered, not even my best friend. I felt so dirty and ashamed. This was 1950. You didn't discuss such actions.

When I was only eleven my mother called me a little whore. I wasn't even sure what it meant then. Now I felt like one.

I realize that my mother had some severe mental and emotional problems. She was insanely jealous of my relationship with Dad. He *was* very affectionate. He called me "Pompy." When he drove the tractor, I would stand behind him with my hands on his shoulders. Mike and I would go barefoot a lot of the time. We'd get jiggers in our toes as a result. Dad would patiently dig them out with needles and a razor blade, taking care not to hurt us too much.

I made friends with a girl on the next-door farm, Pauline. Her boyfriend picked us up one evening to attend a dance at the club. He was Edward, and his friend was Tony. I had a crush on Tony. When it was time to leave, the four of us piled into the front of Edward's truck, me on Tony's lap. My mother had said I was to be home at eleven o'clock, so my friends dropped me off at the end of our driveway. It was a long driveway, so by the time I reached the house, it was five after. Mum was waiting for me. She was furious – said I was late. She started hitting me and slapping my face. I managed to run away from her, ran crying to my room, and locked the door. Shortly after that incident I packed a suitcase and hitched a ride with friends to the big city of Nairobi.

CHAPTER 6

Once in Nairobi, I found a room in the local YWCA. After a few days I started job hunting. I usually took the local bus into town. Quite an experience! The bus was loaded with African *bibis* on their way to the big, open-air market. They were carrying baskets full of bananas, mangos, and papaya. They were great fun, laughing and singing. After a couple of weeks I obtained employment with the advertising department of East African Airways as a receptionist. I learned to type orders. I did enjoy my job and co-workers.

While still on the farm in Kitale, I met a very nice English guy. We started dating. He worked on Lord Lymington's estate. Lymington was related to the Earl of Portsmouth, who was a friend of my brother. Jerry, my new boyfriend, and I eventually became engaged. I was happy with him. He was tall, fair-haired with blue eyes and a nice nature. Shortly afterwards he enlisted in the Kenya Regiment. He was away a lot, hunting down the dreaded Mau Mau terrorists. One day, when Jerry was away, my friend and I were standing in line to attend the cinema. A guy in a posh American car kept driving back and forth and looking at me very intently. He parked his car, walked over to us, and introduced himself. He even asked me for a date; he didn't waste any time. I found him to be quite attractive and very entertaining. I did agree to meet up with him a few days later. He was very slightly dark skinned, and it turned out he was what was known in Nairobi as a "Chi-chi," a half-caste born of an English father and an East Indian mother. It was taboo at that time to fraternize with half-casts. I was not aware of this when I met him. I was captivated by him and eventually we became lovers.

Sadly, I broke off my engagement to Jerry. I know he was heartbroken. Peter was exciting but unpredictable. One evening we were at a popular night-club. I wasn't feeling well and asked Peter to take me home. He ignored my request. A gentleman who'd overheard our conversation came over and offered to take me home. Peter was *furious*. He dragged me down the stairs, shoved me into his car, and started hitting me. That is exactly how my mother would have acted. Unfortunately for him, some of my brother's Kenya Regiment friends witnessed Peter hitting me. They dragged him out of the car and gave him a good hiding. One of them kindly drove me home. There were a few similar incidents. The next month I discovered I was pregnant. What to do?

I had met a tall, blonde English guy, Rusty, who worked for 20th Century Fox Films in a small office across from the New Stanley Hotel. I had broken up with Peter before I discovered I was pregnant. Now I had to tell Rusty of my dilemma. Can you believe that he proposed to me!! It was very gallant of him. I couldn't bear to put him through such an ordeal. Of course I told him that – besides, he couldn't stand Peter. I was only eighteen at the time. It was all a disaster. Peter begged me to move in with him and to have the baby. We discussed the possibility of marriage. He was renting a nice house with a big garden. He was doing quite well as an architect.

My parents had also moved to Nairobi by this time, and Dad had been hired by a large transport company. They were living in a company house and Dad had a small company van. They discovered I was now living with Peter. They were totally dead set against the fact that I may marry him. Then, to my dismay, Mum found out that I was pregnant. She seemed to take it quite calmly, I thought. Little did I know that she had found a lady who performed abortions.

They came to the house. I was now about five months pregnant. The abortionist stuck a long knitting needle up my vagina. She assured me there would not be much pain – more like a very heavy period. WRONG!! She left. A few hours later I did feel a lot of pain. Then I actually gave birth to a tiny, dead baby boy. I was heartbroken. I stayed in bed crying most of the time.

Peter buried him in the garden outside my window. One day his sister was visiting. He took her to the little grave and unearthed the tiny babe to show her. I saw all this through my window! I was mortified! I became very ill and ended up in intensive care in the Nairobi Hospital. Peritonitis was the diagnosis.

After a week I was released from the hospital. My mother came to collect me. She had booked a room for us at the New Stanley Hotel. When we came up to our room after dinner, would you believe it? Peter was in the room, having somehow climbed through the window! We called management and he was escorted out, thank goodness.

Pamela, age 18

CHAPTER 7

I moved in with my parents and started looking for another job. There was a lovely dress boutique called "Adele of Nairobi." I used to go in there occasionally just to look. One day the owner, Adele, asked me if I would model some of her dresses. Of course I said, "Yes, I'd love to!" So she tried various outfits on me, showed me how to walk and pose. There were several girls modeling for her. Sometimes we drove to neighboring towns to put on our shows. Eventually she asked me to work for her. I started the following day. Now I could afford to pay my parents towards my keep.

Modeling for Adele of Nairobi

I started dating Rusty again. One night when leaving a movie, Peter jumped out of nowhere and began attacking Rusty. Luckily some of our friends witnessed this and managed to break up the fight. It was quite frightening and so unpleasant. Peter did eventually marry. They had two children. He had become quite a famous architect and designed the army base in Limassol, Cyprus.

Some years later he called me from Australia. While visiting South Africa he met up with my brother who gave him my phone number. He called to tell me he'd never stopped loving me. All this followed by a long letter giving me his news that he was now retired and spent time on his yacht sailing and enjoying life in Australia.

A lot of movie stars came to Nairobi. William Holden came to make a movie with the French actress Capucine. Rock Hudson and Sydney Poitier were there to film *Something of Value*. Then came Ava Gardner, Clark Gable, and Grace Kelly to star in *Mogambo*. Meryl Streep and Robert Redford came for *Out of Africa*, a true story by Karen Von Blixen of her experiences running a farm in Kenya. One evening I was waiting in the lobby of the New Stanley to meet up with Rusty. I saw Clark Gable coming down the stairs wearing his safari outfit. He was so handsome. He spotted me and gave me a huge wink and a smile. I nearly fainted.

When Rusty arrived we found a table in the lounge. At the next table was Rock Hudson with his "wife" (he'd married his secretary so no one would know he was gay). Sydney Poitier had joined them. The movie they were making was *Something of Value* — the story of an African boy and a white boy growing up together as close friends.

After several months Rusty and I were married. An old friend of mine, a wealthy Italian, paid for our wedding plus gave us a set of crockery as our gift. We had a civil service wedding and then every one of our guests came to our room at the Queens Hotel for a small reception. One of the male guests had a lot to drink. He asked someone to photograph him sitting on the toilet wearing my mother's fancy hat. I don't think it ever ended up in the wedding album. Nine months later I produced a baby girl. We named her Marilyn Janine Elise Hamilton-Paxon. Quite a mouthful!

We rented a house about five miles from Nairobi. I developed chickenpox! That meant that I could no longer breast feed Marilyn. Once I recuperated, I used to push her in her pram a short distance to the bus stop so we could meet Rusty coming home. There were times when he was not on the bus. He'd get a lift much later with a friend he'd been out drinking with. Very disappointing. Marilyn was a good baby; she slept well and hardly ever cried.

When our lease was up we moved to a nice house much further from town. During this time Rusty met up with a group of Americans who worked in the Middle East oilfields. We owned a second-hand car now, so he would stay out late partying with this group at the New Stanley. I never knew what time he'd be home. He was now drinking very heavily. After a few weeks I became very depressed. One evening Dad arrived in the company van. He told me to pack our belongings and to come home with him. I was so happy to see him! He gave up his bedroom for Marilyn and me. My mother had the master bedroom, so Dad slept in a tiny room next to the garage.

Rusty Hamilton-Paxon
My Dad said "He looks like Slim Whitman in the California Desert"

Marilyn was a toddler now. She enjoyed the garden and Dad's goldfish pond. I was now separated from Rusty - not legally, but it was an agreement between us. Through his American friends, he obtained employment in the oilfields. He told me as soon as he was settled he would start sending child support money. I received one check! He used to vacation in Beirut, Lebanon — a lovely city on the coast. This was the era of the fifties.

Rusty and Pam with baby Marilyn

CHAPTER 8

Marilyn was born in 1955. During this time the Mau Mau terrorists were hiding out in the forests. The British government had allowed the Europeans to take over some of the farmlands, parts of which were already being farmed by the Kikuyu (Africans). They tended to attack white settlers on outlying farms. The Mau Mau terrorists were known as "Muingi wa Nagano" – it was an oath of unity. They wanted the whites out of Kenya, which was still a British colony. They conducted oath rituals that involved animal sacrifice, cannibalism, and bestiality. They used broad-bladed machetes ("pangas"), whips, and spears. They tortured their victims including Kikuyus, loyal to the British, who refused to join their movement.

Then came the Lari Massacre. Lari was a Kikuyu village of only ninety men, women, and children. They refused to join the Mau Mau, so they were brutally murdered. Their homes were burned to the ground. The Mau Mau hacked and tortured the bodies of a British family who were discovered on their farm. The young wife was pregnant, the son only six years old.

My aunt and uncle owned a cattle farm on the slopes of Mount Kenya. My aunt wore a gun in a holster around her waist. One day she was watering her roses. She switched the holster to her left hip. Suddenly five Mau Mau appeared, waving their machetes and pangas. She quickly moved her holster to her right hip and started firing. They ran like hell. She wounded one of them. There was a trail of blood in the grass. A few days later my uncle discovered the Mau Mau had hacked all the back legs of his cattle. Their pet cat had been impaled on a fence post. Their loyal Kikuyu houseboy endangered himself by telling them that they were "next on the list to be murdered." They sold their lovely farm and moved to the island of Malta.

Before my aunt and uncle sold the farm, they entertained some interesting guests. My best friend Anna Maria and I were invited to the Nairobi Club to meet the jet pilots off the *H.M.S. Ark Royal*, a British aircraft carrier docked in Mombasa. The pilots were charming; we paired off with Basil and Chris. They rented a car so the four of us explored Nairobi as they were on a week's vacation. They expressed a desire to visit my uncle's farm, so I called them and they invited us all to Sunday lunch. Namyuki, site of the farm, was approximately 120 miles from Nairobi. Basil and Chris took turns driving. You would think they were flying their jet planes. They drove so fast; we were scared and very relieved to reach the farm. The guys loved the farm and the view of Mount Kenya. It was a most enjoyable day; Elsie and Basil were delighted to meet the pilots.

We kept in touch after they left, and a few days later Mum, Dad, Marilyn, and I left for a holiday at the coast. It was so lovely there. The sand was soft and white, so fine, like talcum powder. It squeaked when you walked on it. Dad and I would spend hours snorkeling. The coral reefs were so colorful with hundreds of species of fish. We were invited aboard the *Ark Royal*. Basil treated us to a tour of that enormous ship and later for drinks in the lounge. We were sad to say our goodbyes to such fine and brave young men.

With Basil (from Ark Royal) and Anna Maria Albergetti

Dad in Mombasa

Pam on Ferry on way to Mombasa

CHAPTER 9

I hadn't heard from Rusty for ages. At the local sports club in Nairobi I met a young English guy. He was Frank Lawson. He played rugby and was tall with brown hair. He had an infectious smile. We became good friends. He had a great sense of humor. I loved that about him. As time went on, our friendship turned into a love affair, which lasted a year or so, when out of the blue, Rusty called to say he would be back in Nairobi for two weeks. Could we meet him at the airport in two days? Now Marilyn was four. He'd been gone for two years. I had given up hope of ever seeing him again. And now I cared very deeply for Frank.

Frank Lawson, my boyfriend from Yorkshire, England

Marilyn, age 4

I did have an American boyfriend for a short time before he returned to the States. He was Lance Osswald. He had two young cheetahs as pets. They were very tame and oh, so beautiful. When he returned to New York he took them with him. They loved to ride in the car.

He drove down Fifth Avenue in his topless convertible with the cheetahs on the back seat! He stopped traffic. Pedestrians were craning their necks for a glimpse.

Another time my friend Pat and I took the train from Nairobi overnight to Mombasa for a few days at the Nyali Beach Hotel. One day we were lying on the beach sunbathing when a helicopter buzzed over fairly low; we waved just for fun. This was the last day of our vacation. We were due to board the train that very evening.

To our uttermost amazement, the helicopter landed on the beach next to us!! A handsome American Marine stepped out. He was tall and blonde, white uniform, gold braid, etc. They were off the aircraft carrier docked in the Indian Ocean. Chuck introduced himself and his pilot. He invited us to a dance to be held at the Mombasa Club in honor of the Marines. We, sadly, had to tell him we were leaving on the train that evening. "No problem," he said, "I'll go talk to the station master and change your booking until tomorrow." He later returned to tell us we were all set for the next day!

They called for us in a taxi at seven o'clock and off we went to the Club. We danced the night away and the yanks even taught us how to do the bunny hop. Chuck took us back to the hotel around midnight. He asked me to take a walk along the beach in the moonlight. It was very romantic. He was such a nice guy. Of course, I never saw him again.

So Marilyn and I met Rusty, and we hardly recognized him. We took him home to Mum and Dad's house. They weren't too thrilled to see him. He seemed to assume that this was to be a joyous reunion. I wasn't even physically attracted to him anymore, and I couldn't bear the thought of how hurt Frank must feel.

Frank Lawson's friend, Nick, had this pet buffalo called "Stinkbomb." Frank wanted a photo of me petting him. The only way he would keep calm was if Nick (behind me) would massage his scrotum.

We took the train to Mombasa on the coast. Mum and Dad drove down with Marilyn. We all stayed at the same hotel. Rusty spent most of his time in the bar ogling an attractive blonde "friend" of mine. Finally it was time for him to fly back to the oilfields, this time to Libya. He assured me once he was settled he would find a house to rent in the capital, Tripoli. Then he would send for Marilyn and me. As time went on, he never even sent a postcard.

Eventually I wrote to the company manager to ask him if he knew of Rusty's whereabouts. He responded saying he had no idea where he was. He'd come into the office one day to say he was leaving the company and then completely disappeared. I decided to divorce him on desertion. It took over a year to finalize. I'd lost Frank. He was now dating an airline hostess.

So now I went on a dating binge. The ratio of men to women was seven to one! There was a big selection out there. I was so sad my marriage was over, sad that my mother was so abusive, and devastated that I'd been raped. I didn't seem to care for men, so I treated them with some contempt now. I had so many boyfriends: Georgio, the Italian, Yaagen Trana, the Dane, Herman from Germany, and several English guys. As soon as they showed an interest in me, a serious interest, then I left them. There was Victor. He was in the R.A.F. (Royal Air Force) from England. He was based in Nairobi during the Mau Mau uprising. One night he invited myself and my parents and, of course, Marilyn, to the officer's mess for drinks and dinner. It was a costume party. I went as a tramp. I threw together a scruffy outfit and wore a battered old hat. Well, a lot of the officers wanted to dance with me. They were flirting madly.

Marilyn had fallen asleep in Dad's car. Victor went to check on her. She said he was crying because I was dancing with other men! Marilyn was only about seven. We drove home eventually. Dad had a lot to drink, but he got us home safely. He carried a sleepy Marilyn to her bed and then quietly slipped under her bed and went to sleep!

One night while we were still staying with my parents, getting ready for bed, we heard scuttling noises outside our bedroom window. Marilyn climbed onto my bed which was near the window. Wonder of wonders! There were two lionesses and three small cubs in our garden. What a thrill. The two lionesses were just lying around, but the cubs wanted to play. They chased each other. They jumped all over their mothers who didn't seem to mind. After an hour or so, one of the neighbors had called the police who chased them away using smoke bombs.

We lived across the road from the National Game Park so animals, zebra mostly, and some wildebeest would wander into our garden looking for water during the dry season.

Juma, our houseboy, came on safari with us.

Glen was Mike's best friend—he went on to become a well known White hunter. Unfortunately he was gored by a buffalo which ended his career.

CHAPTER 10

I ended the relationship with Victor. He was terribly upset but due to return to England anyway. A year later he sent me a postcard from Paris.

One night, while enjoying dinner with friends at the New Stanley Grill, the Cabaret artist joined us after his performance. He was Peter Maxwell. Very talented. He had been playing piano and singing and doing imitations of Satchmo and Ella Fitzgerald. He traveled a lot, performing in Las Vegas and different areas of South Africa. He was from England and, of course, performed there as well. He invited me to dinner the following evening. We formed a lasting friendship. He sent me postcards from all over the world.

I had been working for the same company for several years, Commercial Union Insurance Company. I really liked my boss, my co-workers, and the few Africans and Asians who worked there. We had a lot of fun after office hours. If the city hall was putting on a dance, some of us would go join in. One guy, Chris, was Scottish so he'd wear his kilt and teach us all the Highland Fling. After we'd downed a few drinks, we'd drive out to the boss's house, very palatial, and we'd play hockey on the Persian carpets with celery sticks and radishes. I was sad to leave them all. They gave me a real leopard skin purse for a going away gift.

Commercial Union Insurance Co

I had met a nice chap, William Curry, very British, tall with wavy blonde hair, lots of fun. We dated for a while. Meanwhile I was invited to a square dance! It was held in the garden of a home where an American family were living. They had an authentic caller and everyone was dancing and having a grand time. There were Indian ladies wearing their beautiful saris, a few Africans, some of us locals, plus the American hosts, Harold and his wife, Francie. Harold was running Safari Air Services; he used to pick up abandoned baby animals and fly them up to the Mount Kenya Safari Club where William Holden had built an animal orphanage. They were great friends. Francie's brother Eddie had flown from California to explore Africa. He took a shine to me; we would meet for coffee occasionally.

After a while, William Curry proposed to me. I accepted. Time to settle down. Marilyn liked him. His dad said to me, "You'll probably get tired of Curry morning, noon, and night!" I was very fond of his dad. I invited Eddie to meet me for coffee so I could break the news of my engagement. When I told him, he said, "So what are you doing Saturday?!" Sadly William's father died quite suddenly. I got tired of William. He was getting on my nerves. Also, I could tell his mother didn't approve of me. I broke off our engagement.

Brother Eddie, Sister Francie

Francie and William Holden

Now Eddie was pursuing me relentlessly. He took me on safari. I had never been before. I wasn't happy at all about the slaughter of many animals for trophies. The white hunter took me out to look for lions. He spotted one in the bushes. He asked me to get out of the Land Rover and handed me a rifle so I could protect him if the lioness came after him. He stalked the lion and shot him dead. The Africans loaded his great old body into the back of the car. He was triumphant. I was sad. He insisted on taking a photo of me with the poor, dead lion. Eddie had shot a zebra that he was going to have made into a rug and several species of gazelle so he could have the horns mounted. My dad had never killed an animal unless we needed food. Maybe a warthog. We were miles from civilization on the gold mine. The Africans always got their share. I was glad to be home after four days in camp.

Pam and Lion   Lee and Lion

Eddie had been wanting to date me every couple of days. He seemed to be a nice enough guy. I became quite fond of him. One evening in the Long Bar of the hotel, we were enjoying a sundowner, and he sort of proposed to me. I told him I was leaving the following day with Mum and Marilyn for a two-week holiday at the coast. I would think about it and let him have my answer when I returned.

The three of us had planned to leave early next morning but we were so excited, we ended up leaving at eleven o'clock the night before. I drove my little Morris Minor. It was three hundred miles to Mombasa on mostly dirt roads.

We didn't arrive until early morning. We then unpacked and rested. The following morning a taxi pulled up outside our beach cottage. Guess who? Eddie! He was pretty determined to get an early answer from me! He'd bought a bottle of brandy for Mum, which she gladly accepted. I took Marilyn down for a swim while they stayed drinking and apparently planning the wedding…without me!

When we returned it just started happening. Ed's sister, Francie, asked the minister of her church to marry us, which he did in his home. Francie's youngest daughter and Marilyn were our bridesmaids. Anna Maria was my maid of honor. A room was booked at the Norfolk Hotel for us and our reception was held there. I must tell you that my mother had suggested we should have at least one sexual encounter before we married – just in case. "Oh, no," I said. "He wants to wait until we're married." Silly me.

We had a lovely reception surrounded by family and friends. Our wedding cake was beautiful. Champagne and other libations flowed freely. Francie and Harold were there, of course, along with their daughters, Karen and Kimberly, and their son, Eric. I was so busy talking to various guests that I didn't notice that Eddie was drinking a lot. After all the guests had gone, we went off to our wedding night room. Ed tried to make love to me, but it was a disaster.

Eddie loved Africa. He was tempted to stay and perhaps buy a ranch, but the political situation was a bit shaky now that most of the colonial British had left and were no longer ruling the country. The new rulers were very corrupt - taking care of their people was not a priority for them. AIDS was rampant; a lot of Africans died and left orphaned children. Funds donated to the new African government from Europe and the USA were ending up in the rulers' pockets.

CHAPTER 11

Eddie did say he would adopt Marilyn once we got settled in California - it never happened. He also said he would sponsor my parents – that also never happened. However, once I became a citizen, after one year, I did sponsor them. Dad was seventy-two. Even so, within two weeks of his arrival he'd landed a good job on the local golf course. He'd purchased a car and they had found a nice house to rent. I was very proud of them. Dad had to learn to drive on the wrong side of the road. Now it was time for us to leave Nairobi for our journey to California. We took two weeks. Eddie wanted to visit various countries en route. Our first step was Ethiopia. We had friends living there who showed us around. We spent about three days there. Halee Selassic was still the ruler, so the country seemed fairly peaceful.

Next stop: Beirut, Lebanon. In 1964 it was a beautiful and peaceful beach resort. Not any more. We loved it. We stayed two days, walked everywhere, and swam in the warm ocean.

As we walked back to our hotel, a young man driving by offered us a ride. He was on a break from work for a few days. He offered to be our tour guide and would pick us up the following morning. He showed up with his sister, or was she his girlfriend? Never mind; he drove us all over Beirut, to the casino, up in the hills, to a lovely café for Lebanese food, back to the beach, and finally to our hotel. Ed offered to pay him, but he refused. Lovely people.

Our Friends in Beirut

Now we were onto Cairo, Egypt's capital. We visited the *souk* (marketplace) where they sold mostly pure gold jewelry.

Ed had already bought me a beautiful gold ring in Mombasa, and he ordered a bracelet made to match.

We returned to the hotel for lunch and a rest as we planned to attend *Son et Lumiere* (sound and light) show that evening at the pyramids. We were lucky to find seats near the front. The pyramids were lit, and we were astounded by the sight and size of them. There was a narrator with a deep, booming voice over the loudspeaker telling the history of how they were built and the thousands of laborers involved..

As we started to walk back to the hotel around eleven o'clock, there came an Arab leading his camel. He came over to us, lifted Marilyn up onto his camel, and led her around for a long walk. We followed, of course. When he stopped, he lifted her down. Ed held out some money for him, but he just shook his head and bowed to us. What a wonderful experience the night was.

The next day we flew to Athens. We toured during the day and walked up to the Acropolis in the evening. It was magnificent. We found a posh restaurant nearby. Unfortunately, as we were finishing our first course, Marilyn threw up all over the table! Poor little girl. She wasn't used to all the foreign food plus the travel.

Next we got lost trying to find the hotel. We asked a tall young man if he knew the way. He hoisted Marilyn up on his shoulders and led us right to it. It turned out he was a Turkish opera singer!

After Athens we headed for Paris. There was marvelous sightseeing. Mostly we walked, as the old hotel we were staying in was in the center of the city. We saw all the beautiful sights.

From Paris we went to Denmark, then on to Germany – Berlin, in fact. Ed discovered a beer garden. Fatal. We left him there and took a taxi back to the hotel. Several hours later, when we were in bed, he came in with a young German guy. He didn't stay long! I had curlers in my hair and was reading my book. Marilyn was trying to sleep. He was very embarrassed!

Next was Holland and then on to Switzerland. We took a train from Geneva up to the Alps so we could see the snowy mountains. It was thick fog! We couldn't see anything, so we found a theatre and went to the movies.

Finally we took the long flight to Los Angeles. We arrived at night. I was amazed by all the city lights; it seemed to go on forever.

Ethiopia

CHAPTER 12

Ed had sent his mother a postcard of a young topless Masai girl hinting that she was his fiancée. His mother and sister were there to meet us; they both seemed surprised to meet me, a white woman with a British accent and an eight-year-old daughter.

Aunt Shirley drove us over one hundred miles south to Corona Del Mar. We were to stay with Gram, my new mother-in-law. During the drive I was overwhelmed to see huge neon signs advertising funeral homes. Culture shock!

We stayed with Gram for a couple of weeks. She rented a nice two-bedroom house in the lovely beach town of Corona del Mar. She was very hospitable and a great cook, like my mother.

Marilyn started school. It was not a good experience for her. She was teased a lot for her British accent.

We found a place to rent in Newport Beach. The house was situated on a canal. Our landlords, Neil and Phyllis, lived upstairs. They became good friends and sometimes took us out on their boat.

Ed had to do the cooking…I didn't have a clue! Mum cooked for us in Africa, and she had an African cook to help. We also had a houseboy who cleaned house and washed dishes and a *dhobi* (laundry boy) who washed and ironed all our clothes. He even ironed Dad's socks! We had a gardener. We housed them all, gave them food, and paid them wages.

Anyway, I slowly learned to cook and clean and do the laundry. I can't say I enjoyed any of those chores.

Ed was a yacht broker, selling to the wealthy Newport Beach-ites. He was gone all day. Marilyn was in school all day. She was starting to fit in with the local kids. The school was situated on the beach.

I longed to be back at work. I took a bus to Corona Del Mar and found a position in a small travel agency. I rode the bus back and forth; it was tiring. Ed decided it was time for me to have a car. He bought me a tiny Fiat 600 – second hand, but it drove well. I did have to be careful not to drive on the left side as we did in Kenya.

Now Ed decided to quit the yacht broker business. He bought a window covering business in Newport Beach. The owner stayed on and trained both of us how to make window shades – popular window coverings in that era. He took Eddie around to various clients' homes and showed him how to install shades, blinds, and drapes while I stayed in the shop and made the roller shades.

So this was the end of learning the travel business and the end of earning a salary. I discovered I was pregnant. I kept working in the shop as long as possible. We had moved back to Gram's house temporarily as we were planning to rent a two-story house on the beach side in Corona Del Mar.

Luckily, Aunt Shirley and her son Toby were visiting when my water broke and I started labor pains. Toby packed my suitcase, and Shirley got me safely to the car and laid me down on the back seat. She even persuaded the nurse to lend her a cap and gown so she could accompany me to the labor ward!

I wasn't too long in labor. It was a fairly easy, painless birth. Out popped my baby boy. When Ed arrived at the hospital, he'd shaved off his mustache! I asked him why. He said "because our son doesn't have one!" We named him Stephen Ward Wagoner. Once he and I were strong enough, I resumed work at Ed's shade shop. We took Steve's playpen so he would have a place to sleep. When he cried, I was there to cuddle him and give him his bottle.

Pam and Steve

As he grew and started crawling and walking, I asked my neighbor, Pat Abe, to babysit him. She had three children of her own. She was a lovely person. She even taught Steve some Japanese –just two words – *shi-shi* (for needing to pee) and *unko* (for poop). Of course I forgot to mention she and her husband were both Japanese.

By now we were living in a new housing development in Irvine. A few miles inland from Corona Del Mar. Marilyn had to attend school there as there were none in Irvine yet.

We were the fifth family to move into Village One. The local TV station wanted to interview us with the children. They asked Ed to bring some of his African trophies - horns, zebra rug, and other things.

By now Steve was three. He liked to sleep in our bed. If we put him in his room, he yelled bloody murder. Sometimes we'd take him for a car ride. I would hold him and he would calm down and finally go to sleep. This was at two or three in the morning. Once home, I would gently lower him into his bed and say a prayer. As soon as his head touched the pillow, he'd start crying again!

I discovered I was having another baby. This time Gram got involved. She insisted I should stop working and insisted that Ed should have a vasectomy, which she would pay for. Our second son was born July 2nd, 1969. We named him Eric Edward after my father.

Gram, Eric, and Pam

It was not an easy birth. I had a long, painful labor and eventually the doctor discovered it was a breach birth. Eric came out feet first! By now I was screaming bloody murder – as soon as the doc got hold of one foot, he gave me a painkilling shot – *ahhh*, that was better. "Now," he said, "we'll all feel better." I'm just glad he didn't have to do a Caesarean section.

Eric was a delight. He hardly ever cried and smiled a lot. He was very easy to care for. But I was restless. I needed to work. I found an ad in the paper: "Single father with two small children needs a babysitter." I called him; he invited me to come over to meet them all. The girl was close to Steve's age. The boy was slightly older. They were sweet kids. He used to drop them off every morning, plus a load of laundry, and pick them up after work. Steve had fun with them; they got along. Eddie built a playhouse in the backyard, and the kids loved it. Even the neighborhood kids used to come over.

New houses were completed every day; an elementary school, high school, and University of California at Irvine. We made new friends, and the children went to the park every day. There were swings and slides. It was very safe in those days. The kids could come and go in the close neighborhood.

Some years later! Steve, Pam, Eric

CHAPTER 13

The adults had many get-togethers. Usually they were BYOB parties, some costume parties, and, of course, family get-togethers.

My neighbor, Sharon, was the home economics teacher at the high school. Her husband, Guy, was a professor at UCI. They went to Germany on a sabbatical. While there, they adopted four children: the father was Afro-American GI and the mother was a German lady trying to manage the kids alone and quite poor. A while after they arrived home, Sharon became pregnant! She went on to have three more children, so now they had seven! Sharon did a lot of sewing and so did I when I had the time. At Christmas we used to bake cookies together. The children would be seated around a round table. We put bowls of frosting and sprinkles on the table and the cookies for the children to decorate. They had so much fun.

I didn't see Sharon for a while; she came over to visit finally. She said, "Have you heard what happened to Guy?"

I hadn't. She said, "He came out of the closet."

I asked, "What was he doing in there?"

She was angry. "Don't you know what that means?" she asked furiously. I had no clue. She explained that he'd confessed to being gay. He was now living with his boyfriend. Can you imagine? She was now responsible for seven children ages five to sixteen. Sharon and Guy did remain friends, and he never neglected the children. Sharon met a nice man who became her boyfriend.

Now I had some babysitting money so I didn't have to ask Ed for small handouts. He was very sparing with his cash, so I hated to ask him. Ed was drinking more than ever. Why? We had three lovely kids, a nice home, and his dinner would be ready when (or if) he came home. He started making a habit of meeting up with a friend who also drank a lot. I guess he'd lose track of time. One of my girlfriends invited me to the university pub for a drink. Marilyn was old enough to watch the boys now. Ed was not home yet, so I agreed. Before I left, I put some curlers in a scarf and placed it on my pillow, stuffed my nightie with a couple of pillows, and drew the blanket over the lump in the bed. I did sometimes have curlers and a soft scarf when I went to bed.

Off I went to meet my girlfriend. We had a couple of drinks and a chat, and I left to go back home. I walked upstairs to our bedroom. Eddie was sitting up reading a book. He seemed shocked to see me. He did a double-take. He looked down at the pillow and then back at me. He probably thought he was going around the bend. Marilyn was standing in the hallway watching this scenario play out. We were both in hysterics when I pulled the blanket back and Ed finally caught on. By now Marilyn was in her teens; the boys were growing up fast too. Steve was nine and Eric was six.

My dad was ill. I took him to the doctor several times, but he couldn't seem to figure out what was ailing him. He couldn't seem to stay awake. He'd fall asleep in the car on his lunch break. Finally they took blood tests…it was leukemia. Oh, my God. So twice a week to the hospital we went for blood transfusions. Sometimes he'd bring a basket with a bottle of brandy and a soda. On the way home we'd stop at the beach to watch the sunset. It was a precious time for me. Of course he could no longer work. He was bedridden now. He'd worked nearly five years at the golf course. It wasn't long before he had to be hospitalized.

After the children left for school, I would drive about fifteen miles to the hospital to be with him for two or three hours. Mum did come just once. When he saw her, dad said "How was your tennis game?" About a week later Ed told me to wait until he came home from work so he could drive me down to see my dad. Later that morning the doctor called me to say that dad had passed away. On the one morning I didn't visit him! I was heartbroken.

Irvine Women Create 'Kalico Kids Corner'

The innocence of children's things has drawn two Irvine homemakers into the business world with a line of children's clothing, toys and decorative bedroom accessories.

"Touchability" and "color appeal" are the two characteristics of the handcrafted items produced by Pamela Wagoner of University Park and Kaethe Scott of The Ranch.

Their children's world of soft and brightly colored creations is nestled among Newport's unique specialty shops in the Cannery Village on the Newport Peninsula.

The Irvine shopkeepers have named their establishment *The Kalico Kids Corner* and have tucked it in among other boutiques at 2813 Lafayette, Newport Beach. Their brightly colored Raggedy Ann banner flies below the Guildsmerchant sign. They hope to expand in July from the upstairs location to the ground floor of the Guildsmerchant where local artists have displayed custom works in all media.

A first-business venture for both of the Irvine residents, the shop has been open for eight weeks and the owners have been encouraged enough to expand their creations to include custom children's interior decorating. When their expansion is complete, they hope to display several examples of children's room ideas.

Handmade dolls in the another item the "Kalico Kids" produce. Plans are to add several character dolls and to include ethnic dolls such as black, Chinese and Mexican. "These dolls are hard to find and are badly needed," said Mrs. Scott who crafted the three-foot "granny" doll now on display in the shop.

Both shopkeepers have been doing their "crafts" things in the Irvine area for several years. Pam sold some things under the Village Guild, a seasonal boutique which she opened in her home. They also set up a booth in the Arts and Crafts Show of the Irvine Is . . . a Festival in May.

According to Mrs. Scott, the availability of children's things that appeal to youngsters is lagging. "Clothes, toys and other things for children are often designed to appeal to adults," said Mrs. Scott. "We try to capture the colors and attractions that appeal to a child's eye."

Included in their selection of children's things are patchwork quilts, pillows, stuffed animals, wall plaques, Raggedy Ann and Raggedy Andy dolls and wall hangings. Items may be purchased at their shop or may be special-ordered in selected colors and fabrics to coordinate with the child's room.

IRVINE SHOPKEEPERS—*Entering the business world with their children's creations are Kaethe Scott of The Ranch, left, and Pam Wagoner of University Park. Their newly opened shop is called the Kalico Kids Corner of the Guildsmerchant and is located in Newport's Cannery Village at 2813 Lafayette.*

My marriage was falling apart. We no longer had any kind of intimate relationship, and I was really fed up with his constant drinking. I had set my sewing machine up on the table in the garage. My friend Cathy used to come over most days. We made children's clothes, dolls, and stuffed animals. We had decided to open a children's shop in Newport Beach. It was to be named "Calico Kids' Corner." It was a small shop upstairs with a large show window downstairs facing the street. Meanwhile I told Ed I wanted a divorce. We agreed not to hire expensive attorneys. Unfortunately, Gram insisted he hire her lawyer. So of course I had to hire one too.

My mother was staying with us temporarily until she could find a small apartment. I asked Eddie if we could stay in the house until the children were older. "No" was the answer. He wanted to sell it. We'd paid $24,500 ten years prior. Now he listed it with an agent for $58,000. When her listing was up, I told Eddie I would try to sell it myself. He agreed to a couple of weeks. I taped a hand-made sign on the front gate – "House for Sale by Owner. $75,000" Lo and behold, a few days later when we were sewing in the garage, a Mercedes pulled up driven by a man. He got out and asked to see the house. So I showed him around. He asked if we would accept $70,000! I said I would ask my soon-to-be-ex-husband. The man said he was an attorney so he would take care of all of the paperwork. Of course Eddie agreed.

Meanwhile, Cathy and I moved into our shop. We took the sewing machines so we could keep on being productive. One day a friend of mine from Los Angeles came to visit. She was recently divorced but was accompanied by a nice-looking man. They wanted to see our little shop. Then her friend Terry invited Ed and I to his yacht, which was anchored in Newport Beach, for a drink and then dinner in a nearby restaurant.

We met them later on his lovely yacht. Eddie had too much to drink as usual. Terry said, "Let's leave them here, and we'll run over to the restaurant." He was fun. Off we went and were enjoying a pre-dinner drink when Sylvia came rushing in with Eddie staggering behind. Turns out that Terry was a millionaire from Arizona! He was pleased to hear that Ed and I were divorcing. I could tell he was attracted to me, but what about Sylvia?

Ed moved out to a ritzy apartment complex in Newport Beach. I drove Mum all over looking at apartments, but she seemed to find fault with all of them. Now Marilyn was off to college with her girlfriend. It was a long way off, in Lake Tahoe. I managed to find a nice, one-level house. It had three bedrooms and was near the boys' school and all their friends. Mum moved in with us. I gave her the master bedroom. She had her own bathroom. She had severe arthritis in both knees, so if we went out she had to use a wheelchair.

The boys each had their own rooms. And me? I ended up in a small den next to the dining room. We had a small patio where Mum and I could sit in the evenings and enjoy our sundowners. I used some of my share of the sale of the house to open a business in Laguna Beach. It wasn't too long a drive from Irvine. I opened a shade shop. Marilyn was home from college, so I invited her to learn the business. Now what should we call it? Mum said when she was on the stage in London she used to sing "The Shady Lady from Shady Lane." That was it! We called it "The Shady Ladies."

A friend of mine was an interior decorator, so we gave her some leads and she sold some of our window coverings. Marilyn was quite the artist; she would hand-paint flowers and wild animals on the shades. We enjoyed being in that small mall. There were artists and jewelers, a shoe shop, a kitchen shop, and then came an English guy. Frank was his name. He opened a tennis shop. He was a professional tennis player and gave lessons. He became a close friend; I've known him now for thirty-four years.

Ed's shop was a long way from ours. He used to visit occasionally and even did some installations for us.

CHAPTER 14

Going back to the time before Dad died...eventually the doctor had advised that he live at the hospital. Dad was hooked up to IV machines. If he needed the restroom he never called for a bedpan; instead he got up and dragged the machines with him into the bathroom. Pride personified. I would see the boys and Marilyn off to school then drive from Irvine to South Laguna every morning to see him. I sat by his bed and told him all the family news. He hardly responded. I told the doctor, "I don't think he can hear me."

He was cremated and interred in a niche at a beautiful funeral home in Corona Del Mar. I later took his ashes with me to South Africa. My brother, his wife, and I scattered his ashes on the Blyde River, near the town of Pilgrim's Rest, his most favorite place in the world.

While we were still married, Ed had a friend, Winnie Anderson, who also lived in Newport Beach. He owned a timeshare condominium on the island of Maui, Hawaii. He invited us there to spend a vacation with him. His girlfriend, Dixie, would be joining us a few days later. It was situated on the beach and we could walk across to a Sheraton Hotel, swim in their huge pool, play in the ocean, and enjoy dining there occasionally. Before Dixie arrived, Winnie used to dump his laundry on my bed. The laundry room adjoined our room, so I didn't mind doing his washing together with ours. One day I decided to play a trick on him. I sewed up the fly on his boxer shorts. We wondered when he would discover it.

Eddie and Pamela Wagoner

My parents

My brother, Mike

Dixie arrived, and two days later we flew to the beautiful island of Kauai to stay a couple of days. One night, after we'd dined in the hotel, Dixie and I paid a visit to the ladies' room. Ed and Winnie went off to the men's room. Ed heard Winnie cursing and shouting – he'd finally worn the sewn-up boxer shorts! He was in quite a state, of course. When he found out I was the culprit, he chased me a long way along the beach! Kauai was so beautiful; we explored the whole island before returning to Maui.

We decided one summer to drive to Yosemite National Park to camp out. We purchased a tent and sleeping bags. Steve was three. Marilyn was eleven. I had brought a large honey-baked ham, plus potatoes, veggies, bread, and other sides. That would keep us all going for a few days. The first day we erected the tent next to a picnic table. Ed took the kids horseback riding. Later we had a pleasant evening around the campfire roasting marshmallows. We had the Styrofoam cooler on the picnic table packed with all our food, including the ham. We set a large rock on top of the cooler. During the night I heard noises nearby. I woke Ed. He said it was probably raccoons. He went back to sleep. I crept out of the tent in my nightie. It was a clear moonlit night. The lid was off the cooler! The rock was on the ground. Then I saw a young bear running on three legs with our ham under his arm! So I gave chase. I guess I was shouting because a man came out of his tent. He asked, "What are you doing?"

I said, "Chasing that bear! He stole my ham!"

The guy asked loudly, "Are you crazy, lady?"

I slowly made it back to the tent, feeling very disappointed. We were at a high altitude in those hills. In the morning Marilyn developed a gushing nosebleed. We wrapped towels around her face and drove straight to the fire station. The firemen were very helpful and immediately gave her oxygen and even let us take a canister back to our campground. Quite an adventurous trip.

Mother came to stay until we could find suitable accommodations for her.

CHAPTER 15

Meanwhile, Terry flew me to La Paz in Mexico where his boat was now anchored. There was another couple who joined us - a married man with his mistress. It was a lovely sail; we visited uninhabited islands and went ashore to explore. We sailed for miles. Terry did some fishing. It was a dream trip. One day Terry was in our home visiting and meeting my mother, Steve and Eric. Suddenly Ed dashed in, muttering that he'd forgotten something. He was quickly up the stairs and down again, then out the front door. Evidently he called Sylvia to tell her Terry was visiting. After he'd left, I got a call from Sylvia. She was still seeing him. Apparently he had a wife and son! Wow! That was a shock.

Off the coast of Mexico   Two-timing millionaire from Arizona

Terry told me later that his wife didn't care what he did in his spare time as long as he was home on Sundays to take her to church! Here I was thinking he was the love of my life, but who could know what he was up to? A week later he invited Cathy, (my partner at Calico Kids' Corner), her friend, and me to his ranch near Phoenix. I agreed. Cathy was so excited, but I had an ominous feeling about the trip. Anyway he flew the three of us to Phoenix, collected us, and drove to a small hotel – one floor – with a nice big pool. He had two brothers who were waiting there. We all played tennis for a while, then changed into our riding gear and went horseback riding. Then we went back to the hotel for a swim. Terry had hired a masseuse for us all. All this time I noticed him making a play for Cathy. She'd had a boob job, so they were BIG. She was quite attractive. She was short with fiery red hair, but her eyes were too small and close together, in my opinion. When she was having her massage in another room, Terry disappeared. I took a shower and wrapped in a towel to wait for my massage. Suddenly, Terry's younger brother burst into our room. He wanted to have sex with me!

It was then that I realized what the game was. Terry was probably screwing Cathy. I declined the massage. Dinner was delivered to our rooms. I refused to make love with Terry that night. We flew back to California the next day. Next time Terry called me, I told him I no longer wanted to see him. He argued that he wanted to buy a house in Bermuda for me and my two boys. I told him my friendship with Cathy was over. She'd been outrageously flirting with him in Phoenix. I told him that I knew he was still seeing Sylvia, that she had been a good friend of mine. So he said, "I'll buy you a ranch in Arizona, then you and Sylvia can live there with your kids!"

He called me several times. He eventually realized that I was through with him. Oh, well…it was fun while it lasted. We closed our business. Cathy went off with some guy on the back of his motorbike. She left her husband in the lurch!

CHAPTER 16

I found work in a dress shop on Balboa Island. Ed used to come by to see the boys, or he would take them up to Big Bear Mountain for ski lessons. He now had an attractive blonde girlfriend. She had also left her husband.

Now my brother was living near Durban in South Africa. One day I overheard my mother calling him to say I was being unkind to her. My God! I used to take her shopping, to the library, cinema, anywhere she wanted to go. She got to meet all my friends. Each time we went out, I had to lift her heavy wheelchair into the trunk of my car. I couldn't believe what she was saying. She told me later that Mike had said, "Come to South Africa! We'll find you an apartment near our condo."

Marilyn and I helped her pack and got lost driving to Los Angeles Airport. We eventually arrived. Mother was late but the attendants rushed her through. PHEW! That was a close call! Marilyn and I were dizzy with delight. Mum survived the long plane flight but her luggage came on a later plane. It didn't seem to bother her; she was seventy-eight years old. Brave lady. The flight to South Africa is twenty-six hours!

About a week after her arrival she was safely installed in her apartment. Mike called me and said, "I'm sending her back on a one-way ticket!"

I said, "Mike, I had her for six years!" Well, about two years later I did go to visit them all in South Africa. Los Angeles to Pinetown, twenty-six hours flying time. It took me two days to get over the jet lag.

Witch Doctor, Pilgrim's Rest, South Africa Lady with her babe

Beach, Durban, South Africa

Mum in Durban, 1959   Weaving

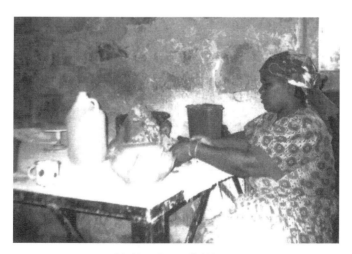

Making Beautiful Vases

Bush Camp

Ardmore

The Bazaar, South Africa

Kruger National Park, South Africa

Marilyn

Eric

CHAPTER 17

I stayed with Mum in her small apartment. In the evenings we'd have our sundowners of brandy and soda, and I would get my notebook out and ask her to tell me some highlights of her life onstage in London. One evening, actually New Year's Eve, Mike came to tell us he was driving us downtown as there was to be a parade.

The parade was wonderful. African dancers in tribal dress and painted faces were singing and whistling. Mike had brought a large cooler full of drinks. A young man on a motorbike offered to take Mum for a ride. We got her out of the wheelchair and somehow onto the back of his motorbike, side saddle. He took her for quite a long ride. She was very thrilled.

When I returned to California I could no longer afford the rent for the house without the financial help from Mum. So we were on the move again. This time we were in a ground floor apartment with three bedrooms, also close to the boys' schools. Steve was now attending University High School - he was fourteen. Eric, at age eleven, was still in Irvine Elementary School. I had used my share of the profits from selling the house to open my own window covering business in Laguna Beach. Marilyn was back from college and living with a boyfriend, so I brought her into the business and taught her how to make the window shades. As I stated before, we called our shop "The Shady Ladies." The sales rep we hired travelled all around California drumming up business. We also hired a lovely Irish gal to work with us, as well as an interior decorator. We were so busy that we rented a separate work room. The orders were coming in fast!

Pam's son Steve

CHAPTER 18

Remembering Robin Williams

It was in the early seventies that I first saw him at the Laugh Stop, a comedy club in Costa Mesa, California. He was a little known stand-up comedian at that time.

I was with friends, dining and drinking and feeling great. We were seated near the stage. Robin was performing a Shakespeare skit, reciting while walking across the stage carrying a lighted candle that kept blowing out. He called me up on stage to walk with him and re-light the candle each time it blew out. At the end of his act he thanked me, and I returned to my seat.

When he re-appeared on stage, his act was hilarious. He had everyone in hysterics, laughing to the point of tears. He did an imitation of a female Russian gymnast during an interview by an American reporter. He was talking fast and his accents were perfect.

After the show I went back on stage to congratulate him. I remember telling him, "The next time I see you, you will be famous!" As we were conversing, an agent from Rowan & Martin's *Laugh-In* show approached him. I said my farewell and left.

A short time later we heard that he would be appearing again at Laugh Stop. My teenage daughter wanted to see him. As we were leaving, my ex-husband showed up. He wanted to accompany us. I was apprehensive as I could tell he'd already had a few drinks. He was insistent. Off we went to see Robin perform. As he began, my ex started heckling him, calling out derogatory remarks. Robin didn't seemed to be bothered - he mostly ignored Ed or came back with clever comments. My daughter was embarrassed, ashamed, and crying. We retreated to the back of the room. The bouncer was hovering there. We asked him if he intended to escort my ex to the door, but the bouncer said, "No, Robin can handle him. He knows what to do. He'll give me a sign if necessary." My daughter would no longer stay in the room. She left to wait in the car. When the show was over I went to apologize to Robin. I explained my daughter was so upset that she was waiting in the car. He insisted on coming out to see her. He was so kind and sympathetic to her. He told her not to worry, that it often happened. Then my drunken ex staggered out. He said, "Hey, Robin, how about you come back to the house for a couple of drinks?"

Robin said, "No, thanks, I've got to get home to feed my baby parrot. He needs to nurse every four hours!"

Some weeks later my son called me. "Mom, come see, Robin Williams is on TV." I believe it was a *Laugh-In* segment and then, of course, came *Mork & Mindy*, followed by many movie roles.

I'll end my story by saying he was a lovely man with such an imaginative sense of humor and a talent unequalled. He will be so missed worldwide. He was a ray of sunshine in our lives.

CHAPTER 19

Ray Ryan

E d was leaving on a fishing trip for the weekend. His sister, Francie, invited me to Palm Springs. We would stay overnight with Helen Ryan, wife of Ray. He, William Holden, and Carl Hirschman purchased Mawingo, a hotel situated at the base of Mount Kenya in Nanyuki. They had planned a hunting safari. One of their professional hunters was Terry Mathews. I knew him, since his wife was a friend of mine. They fell in love with the area and decided to go in partnership and made an offer to purchase the Mawingo Hotel. Jack Block owned the hotel. He also owned the New Stanley Hotel in Nairobi. They reached an agreement on price.

Ray Ryan decided to turn the hotel into a resort for the rich. New wings were constructed. A heated outdoor swimming pool was installed. The dining area was expanded. Horse stables were built, along with a bird sanctuary. Read *Mob Murder of America's Greatest Gambler* by Herb Maryneu with Steve Baybery for details of Ray Ryan's life and death. Hirschman brought in top chefs from Europe. A large vegetable garden was planted. My Aunt Elsie, who owned a farm nearby, planted an herb garden at William Holden's request.

Now it became The Mount Kenya Safari Club. I was lucky enough to visit a few times. It was such a beautiful setting. Ray described it as heaven on Earth.

Mt. Kenya Safari Club

Chuka dancers entertaining the guests

When Francie and I stayed with Helen Ryan in their beautiful home in Palm Springs, Helen took us to her private club for dinner. Francie's husband owned Safari Air Services. He used to fly orphaned animals to the Mount Kenya Safari Club where William Holden had installed an animal orphanage. After Ray Ryan was murdered, Helen had him cremated, then flew to Kenya and scattered his ashes over the area. Africa was his love.

Orphaned animals flown to the Club orphanage by Safari Air Services

CHAPTER 20

At our Shady Ladies shop, Marilyn and I had a lot of expenses and not too much profit, but we managed to pay for our housing and food plus some extras. The business survived for fifteen years! Now Steve was fifteen, in high school and a member of the school soccer team. A huge soccer rally was held in California, with high schoolers coming from different parts of the world. The parents were asked to host the international teams and their coaches. We hosted two of the players. We took them to Disneyland. They were so excited. All the boys got on so well, and the coaches made Cuba Libres for us adults one evening.

A month or so later, after everyone had left, we received an invite to Ecuador and Peru. In order to raise enough money for the boys' team plus the coaches' airfares, we held bake sales and car washes galore. Braniff Airlines was still operating at the time. They very kindly gave me a free fare as the "Team Mother" and reduced fares for the boys. Ed decided to make the trip with Eric, who was about twelve at the time. Several of the other parents came along.

It was a long flight to Peru. We stayed in a hotel in the town center of Lima. Upon arrival, they insisted we drink tea made from cocoa leaves (cocaine, I guess) because of the very high altitude. Otherwise we could become quite ill. I doubt that Eric drank his tea because our tour guides had to give him oxygen. There seemed no age limit for alcohol. At the bar in the evenings, a few of the boys shared a beer then went to the town square to practice their soccer.

The Peruvian team wiped the floor with our American boys. Of course, they were more used to the altitude! We did quite a bit of sightseeing. Lima, the capital of Peru, is a lovely town. I asked our appointed tour guides if we could take a trip to Machu Picchu, so they arranged everything. We all piled onto the train and zig-zagged up through the mountains to this incredible ancient city. Some Peruvian boys were running alongside the train, actually racing it! They had good, strong lungs. When we arrived, I found it to be simply breathtaking. It is called the Lost City of the Incas. Steve and two of his friends were not too interested in taking the tour and asked if they could go climb hills instead. The rest of us had an interesting tour and returned to the train dog-tired, having done a lot of walking. It was my job, of course, to count all the boys to make sure no one got left behind.

The next stop was Quito, capital of Ecuador. We were met at the airport by some of the Ecuadorian team and their parents, who drove us to the various homes where we'd be hosted. Eddie and I were hosted by a lovely middle-aged widow with ten children; of course, her children were mostly grown up and leading their own lives. Paco was still at home. He was a team member, fourteen or fifteen years old. The Ecuadorians were wonderful hosts. They seemed to really enjoy life in those days. I'm talking about the eighties. They had parties for us with food, drinks, and dancing. The boys even danced with their grandmas! Our American boys gaped open-mouthed. I don't think any of them would dream of even dancing with even their *mothers*!

We toured Quito, of course. The churches were incredible, mostly covered in gold leaf. Beautiful statues. I purchased a Panama hat in the shopping district, which Steve wore to his high school graduation with his all-white tux. He was a knockout! Steve was hosted by a very wealthy family. He was delighted that the maids even tied his shoelaces!

After a hectic, wonderful week in Quito, it was time to say goodbye. On the last night, they organized a marvelous party for all of us in a private home. The boys were sent to play in the large backyard. Unfortunately, they discovered an old still back there and proceeded to mix the liquor with their soft drinks. The Ecuadorian boys persuaded the American team to remove license plates from the adults' cars; some were diplomats. They were eventually retrieved except for one; the boy had it in his backpack. It wasn't until we arrived at the airport in the morning that it was discovered. Thank goodness. We left on a rather sour note.

In the plane on the way home, I noticed one of the boys was stuffing chunks of green grass in his backpack. "What are you doing?" I asked suspiciously.

"I'm feeding my lizard!" It was an iguana.

I said, "You'll never get through customs." But he did! I couldn't believe it.

The following day his mother called me. "Why did you let my son bring that horrible creature home?" He must have gone climbing the hills of Machu Picchu. In time, she grew very fond of his iguana. It kept growing, and eventually they had to donate it to the zoo.

CHAPTER 21

Even though we were now divorced, Eddie and I were playing tennis every few days. We were getting quite good. We joined a tennis team – there were about twenty-five lovely people on the team. We were all invited to play in Tahiti and Fiji. Tony Trabert (the famous Aussie tennis player) and his wife, plus Geoff Edwards, the radio announcer, were to accompany us. We had a grand time. Tahiti was so lovely; we enjoyed swimming and snorkeling. We gathered together in the evenings for drinks and dinner.

Now remember - Ed and I had been divorced quite a few years, but we were okay sharing a room. I believe Eddie still loved me, but he had a difficult time showing his feelings. In spite of his day-to-day mean streak, he was very generous when it came to travel, and once in a while he'd come home with a lovely dress or little fur jacket for me. When he did this, I was completely surprised.

From Tahiti, we were bussed to Fiji. The bus was crowded. Some of the men sat on suitcases in the walkway. It was raining cats and dogs! Can you believe it? We passed a soccer field, and there were young boys playing soccer barefoot! In the pouring rain!

We arrived at our hotel in the early evening. It was time to shower and change for dinner. The next day our tennis tournament started. My partner hadn't been playing for long, but he was fast and great at the net. We did well. It was all mixed doubles. Ed had an attractive blonde partner. We played for four days. The last night was a gala and prize giving. Ed and his partner won the first prize trophy presented by Tony Trabert. My partner and I won second! The best for me was that Tony learned forward and told me, "You are beautiful!" That really made my day.

I made some new friends in Tahiti   Tennis in Fiji

Leaving Tahiti

The next day was the long flight back to California and back to work at the shop. When we returned from Fiji and Tahiti, members of the tennis team who lived in the Los Angeles area decided to have a reunion party. Two members, a married couple, offered to drive us. Ed drove up from Lake Forest and left his car at my house. We had a great time at the party; it was fun to meet up with our friends again. Unfortunately, both our husbands had too much to drink. The wife had to drive. She and I sat in the front. When we arrived at my house we turned around to let the men know we were home and would you believe it... they were kissing!!! French kissing! We were shocked.

She was very upset. They had children. I guess her husband left her to live with a gay man he knew, and they eventually divorced. Of course, Ed and I were already divorced, but it was all very confusing.

CHAPTER 22

Now, since Eddie and I seemed to be getting along quite well, he suggested that we try to reconcile. I gave it some thought – maybe it would be better for the boys? I wouldn't have to worry so much about the finances.

Ed leased out his house in Lake Forest and rented a three-bedroom house back in Irvine, close to the boys' schools. The day we moved in, I felt I had made a terrible mistake. We couldn't agree on how the furniture should be arranged for a start, and from then on I just let him have his own way. I still drove to Shady Ladies in Laguna Beach every day. I really enjoyed the creative aspect of it all. Plus, I got to see Marilyn at home, though it wasn't going so well.

I became very depressed. Steve got into trouble (he was actually an innocent bystander but the cops nabbed all the boys). One of them was eighteen so he actually ended up in jail. The other two were sixteen and seventeen, so they ended up in juvenile hall. I was devastated. When we were allowed to visit Steve, he begged us to try and get him released. He said he had to clean the bathrooms and scrub the floors. I talked to Ed about finding an attorney who may be able to help. He wasn't interested in even discussing it.

I found an attorney in Laguna who thought he may be able to help the two boys. His fee was high, but I went ahead and paid him. He managed to obtain their release in a couple of days, but they had to be under house arrest for ten days.

Steve was very popular with the girls. They used to visit him, even clean and tidy his room while he reclined on his bed drinking Coke. One morning I went to his room to have a chat. He was nicking his wrists with a razor blade! Now I knew for sure something was very wrong. He was sometimes in a terrible mood and would punch holes in the wall and take out his temper on his younger brother, Eric. Ed refused to even consider counseling. Once again, it was up to me.

I found a lady counselor for him. He would see her once a week. He liked her; they got on well together, but after six sessions I realized she was more of a friend than an advisor. Once again, I was responsible for a high fee. Ed and I discussed the fact that the reconciliation wasn't working. He wanted to take the boys back to his home in Lake Forest. We would give up the rented place in Irvine. I was broke. The attorney fees plus the counselor fees had dried up my little savings account. I was no longer able to rent a place for the boys and me.

I found a smaller studio in Laguna Beach. It was attached to the main house. There was a small kitchen area and a tiny bathroom. I would be sleeping on a pullout bed. The owners of the home became dear friends - Bob and Emma. I'll never forget their kindness towards me. There was a huge patio, plus a Jacuzzi. Often, when I came in from work, they would invite me for a drink and a home-cooked dinner. The boys were not happy in Lake Forest. They hated their new schools. Steve would get up a five in the morning and catch the bus back to his high school in Irvine!

CHAPTER 23

A s time went on, I started saving again. I did want to see my mother, who was living in South Africa at this time, not far from where my brother and his wife lived. I checked into all the airfares and then my Chinese friend Cherry called me from the island of Cyprus. She said, "Come and see me on your way to South Africa!!" It was hardly on the way.

I called the airline; they said they would only charge twenty-five dollars extra. I said, "Let's do it!" Little did I know this excursion would change my life quite dramatically. Cherry had sold all her restaurants by now. She was living in a nice apartment in the center of town. She came to meet me at the Nicosia Airport dressed in a cheongsam and leopard coat. She was in the company of a young British preacher. He drove us to her apartment. She and I sat talking late into the night. She said, "By the way, we're invited to dinner with my Austrian friends to-morrow. We'll have drinks, and later we'll go to the Chinese restaurant."

The following evening we took a taxi to our friend Christine's house. There were two other visitors - a friendly young man and an older man sitting in a chair looking rather grumpy. Apparently Cherry had told Christine that she was bringing her friend from California, a divorcee. When Ralph (the grumpy one) heard this, he said, "I want nothing to do with her; she'll have blue rinse hair and be living on her ex-husband's alimony."

Well, I came sauntering in, my red hair gleaming, wearing my little black dress, with not one cent of alimony! Suddenly, I found Ralph sitting next to me at dinner and inviting me out the following evening. He was a charming older Englishman, semi-retired to Paphos, Cyprus. He was very interesting and well-travelled. He'd worked for White Horse Whiskey for many years. He told me he'd set up an office in his apartment and was still working for them part-time, mornings only. He had a great sense of humor, and I felt quite attracted to him.

My dear friend Cherry. Retired now and living in Nicosia, Cyprus. She had owned Pagoda restaurants in Nairobi, where William Holden used to hang out. She also owned restaurants in Beirut and Athens.

Ralph Goodman

He picked me up from Cherry's apartment the following evening and took me to a nice hotel for dinner. Unfortunately, the bar did not stock his favorite white wine, Palomino. He was very annoyed and proceeded to drink quite a few anyway. In fact, he got rather drunk. Oh no, not again; not another alcoholic! Eventually we had dinner. He took me home by taxi. I agreed to have lunch with him the following day. He insisted we should all drive down to Paphos to pay him a visit, which we did in the next couple of days. I learned that he'd also been married and divorced and had a lot of female "friends." His apartment was nicely furnished with many mementos collected on his world travels. There was a large balcony where we'd sit to admire the Mediterranean view. He was by my side all the time, whispering sweet nothings in my ears.

It was a treat for me, I must admit. I was forty-eight and had been divorced for twelve years. I had had no serious romantic involvements. There was a slight shortage of eligible men in California. If they were close to my age, they were looking for twenty-five year olds. A few days later I was off to South Africa. Ralph wanted phone numbers and an address. Once I arrived there, he called me constantly and wrote long, loving letters.

He asked me to visit him in Cyprus again on my way home. I agreed, and he was there to meet me when we touched down in Larnaca. It was fairly late when I arrived, so we had drinks and dinner. He had a lot to drink. When we went to our room he suggested I might like an early night. I was tired; it had been a long flight. I got ready for bed. He decided to go back down to the bar for a nightcap. Many hours later he woke me when he staggered into our room. He was falling all over the place. I was quite upset. He even climbed into my bed and tried unsuccessfully to make love to me! I was relieved when he finally gave up and went to sleep.

I spent a pleasant week with Ralph in Paphos. At around noon every day his secretary would come into the kitchen and pour a glass of Palomino wine for him. This would be repeated several times until office closing time at one in the afternoon. I sometimes prepared lunch, or we would drive down to the Hondros Restaurant and enjoy their delicious Greek food. Plus, of course, more Palomino. After lunch Ralph would collapse for his siesta for several hours. I was beginning to feel uneasy about the quantity of wine and, some-times, whiskey that was consumed. But I was spellbound by his charm and generosity, his lovemaking, and the many beautiful poems he wrote.

CHAPTER 24

In any case, it was time for me to return to California and the shop. Back down to earth again. The time I'd spent with Ralph was just the beginning, as far as he was concerned. He called me every few evenings, plus there were endless love letters. I must admit, I was beginning to fall for him.

He sent me airline tickets every few months to have me visit him for a week or so. This went on for several months until we decided to live together in Cyprus. It was an island I had grown to love. The beauty of the beaches and surrounding countryside dazzled me. We were on the Greek side - the Turks had invaded Famagusta and Kyrenia and taken over half of the island.

He invited Steve, my older son, to come for a visit with his girlfriend and sent them the return airfares. They loved the island. At Christmas we used to drive up to the Troodos Mountains for several days with friends from Limassol and Nicosia. It was so beautiful. There was a lovely hotel, swimming pool, and lovely scenery. He even sent tickets to Steve and his younger brother, Eric, to come spend Christmas with us all. He rented a small apartment for them. One day the boys and I rented bikes and rode from the beach apartment in Paphos south along the coast. On the way there, was a small cold drink stand. We stopped to buy Cokes. No one was tending shop, but there was a dish with some coins and a note stating prices and asking customers to put the money in the dish! My California boys were amazed.

Curium Outdoor Theatre

Ladies of the Village, Cyprus

Ralph would send me home every few months to see Marilyn and the boys and to catch up with old friends. At this point Marilyn and Louise were running the shop. I had turned it over to Marilyn. Sometimes Steve or Eric would be required to install window coverings.

When Ralph had to go to London on business for a few days, I would sometimes accompany him. We'd stay at the Sloane Club. He'd been a member for several years. It was pretty much central London. Ralph took me to a beautiful store, September, and gifted me with a beautiful embroidered top, a matching purse, and a belt, plus a cream silk skirt.

From London, we flew to Bordeaux, France to stay with French friends of Ralph. They were an interesting couple. They took us to Cap-Ferrat on the coast, and while there, we were all invited aboard their friends' yacht. It was a lovely, sunny day, so we wore our swimsuits, jumping in for a swim to cool off. Philippe (Ralph's friend) was a bit naughty, barging into the room when I was changing into night attire. Ralph was still in the dining room talking to Monique - in French, of course. I wasn't too sure what was going on but managed to politely show Philippe to the door.

CHAPTER 25

I forgot to mention that Ralph was born in Alexandria, Egypt. He grew up speaking fluent French, Arabic, and English. His late father was a Polish Jew. He was hired by British intelligence – MI6 (equivalent of the CIA, I suppose). They set him up as a German watchmaker in Berlin. He spoke fluent German. He spied for the British and was actually captured a couple of times and imprisoned, but he managed to escape. Ralph's mother was purebred British. She also worked for MI6. She was stationed at a British army base in Larnaca, Cyprus.

Now Ralph also became involved. He was stationed in Cairo. The house they provided had a special secret exit in case he needed to disappear in a hurry. At the time, King Farouk ruled Egypt. Ralph heard through the grapevine that he was to hold a secret meeting in an off-limits building. He took two of his aides to bug the meeting room. They had to sneak in secretly and nearly got caught and arrested on their way out. A couple of days later when they listened intently to their recordings, all they could hear were small children playing and laughing and asking the teachers to take them to potty. They'd wired the day nursery instead of the VIP meeting room! Ralph never told me any of the important MI6 adventures. He was sworn to secrecy, after all.

He had business meetings in the UAE. We stayed at a lovely little hotel in Sharjah. We visited a friend of his in Oman who took us out sailing in his catamaran. Through his business associates, we met the ruler of Oman's nephew. He took us to the museum that was full of Omani antiquities. He told Ralph and I to each select one of the pieces. There were so many of great value that we were embarrassed to take anything. I took a small saddlebag and Ralph selected a long, cotton kaftan. There were three carloads of us, and we drove out to see the countryside. The nephew took us to his country villa, complete with swimming pool. The women were not allowed in the pool with the men. We had to wait our turn!

Hotel in Sharjah, U.A.E.

With the Ruler of Oman's nephew

At his country villa

Market Place, Oman

Beautiful Oman

Oman

Oman

On the way to the villa

CHAPTER 26

S everal weeks later we met up with him in Nice. He took several of us by
motorboat out to his friend's yacht. The nephew was a handsome young
man with good manners. He did not wear his thobe kaftan in the South of
France. He wore a suit and tie.

Venice

Nice, South of France

The following year we took a cruise. It included the ancient ruins of Ephesus along the Turkish Coast. Ralph stayed on the ship – at the bar, of course – but I took the tour of Ephesus. It was a hot day and a long, dusty bus ride, but we had a very knowledgeable guide. It was a memorable tour.

We sailed on to Istanbul. There was marvelous sightseeing, including the Blue Mosque and stories of the long ago prince's harem. The ship was staying in port for a few days, so I took a boat tour across the Bosphorus. It was a beautiful day, and I met some interesting people. There was a German guy who seemed to have a crush on me. He followed me everywhere.

Our next port of call was Athens. Ralph contacted a close friend of his who lived there. He drove us all over Athens on a wonderful tour. He knew exactly what to show us and later came aboard to join us for dinner. The following day we took a cab to the airport and flew home to Paphos. We did finally marry. Ralph proposed the night before I was to leave for California to visit my children and a few old friends. I told him I would think about it and let him know on my return two weeks later.

CHAPTER 27

Marilyn and Louise were still running the Shady Ladies, but Marilyn was preparing it for sale as her husband wanted to move to Seattle. I stayed with Louise. She was alone now. She was divorced, and her two teenage daughters had chosen to stay with their father. Louise had been diagnosed with cancer. She was a beautiful Irish lady with red hair and sparkling blue eyes. I was heartbroken. We had so enjoyed working with her for several years. She had decided to sell her house in Laguna Beach in order to be close to her mother who lived about fifty miles inland. I offered to drive her there. Shortly after we set off, she decided to lie down on the back seat. I took a peek at her. She was fast asleep and slept all the way to our destination. Apparently she only lived for a few months after moving. Marilyn and I really loved her. It was a great loss.

Louise, the lovely Irish gal who worked with us at the Shady Ladies

CHAPTER 28

I found a small building just down the hill from our villa in Cyprus. Just two rooms, unfurnished. I found a couple of old tables and two rickety chairs. This little building belonged to our landlord, so he let me have it for nominal rent. I made it into an art studio. Our cats used to come down and bask in the sun. When Ralph took his long siesta after lunch, I would head for the studio. A few of my friends from our art class would join me. We had great fun painting and sharing ideas and various mediums. I displayed some of my hand-sewn wall hangings and soft sculptures at an art gallery in town and earned some pocket money.

Eventually we were invited to hold an exhibition at the Kyklos Gallery in Paphos to be opened by Mr. Costas Economou. We selected a few of our favorite paintings to display. The exhibition lasted ten days. We sold several paintings.

You are invited

to an exhibition of International Women's Art

"INSPIRATIONAL REPRESENTATIONS»

The exhibition will be opened

by Mr. **Costas Economou**

at the "KYKLOS" Gallery Paphos

on Saturday 5th March 1994, at 7.30 p.m.

Duration : 5.3.94 - 15.3.94

KYKLOS GALLERY
Tel. 06-236681 PAPHOS

Open daily : 9.00 a.m. - 12.00 m.
: 3.00 p.m. - 6.00 p.m.

WHERE!: A soft sculpture by Pamela Goodman, of Paphos, looks for a salon to rest his weights.

Soft sculpture

Pamela Goodman makes magnificent soft sculptures. Not toys, but art, like Claus Oldenburg, who even went as far as typwriters.

Pamela is now working on at least 20 pieces and is up to her scales on a large mermaid. Some of you will recognise her work from, the late Andy Hadjiadamou' book. Her weightlifter is on the cover. Such welcome images on the Cyprus art scene.

Pamela lives in Paphos and these wonderful pieces are quietly waiting to rest in a most suitable gallery. They could fill Gloria's, nudging in good humour; spread out at Diaspro; loll around at Apocalypse up and down those circular stairs; fill Argo; surround Argo; face the Window at Alinea; curl up at Obelisk or even crawl up the Venetian walls at Famagusta Gate (Costas will look after them, I'm sure).

And, what about Limassol? A soft sculpture ball at Peter's marble halls. Smiling in the xvli at Morphi. I can imagine them ensconced at Kyklos, Paphos, can't

you? Looking out to sea or enticing the tourists into the old carob house. Or, what about that distinguished art gallery belonging to the Popular Bank at Paphos?

I can see them holding onto the brass rails at Amathus Beach Hotel, all cushy against metal and marble, by the indoor pool, reflected in the glass and on that luscious green grass that is forever Paul Veronese.

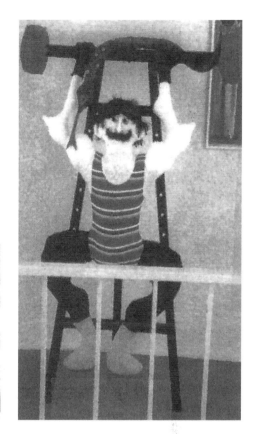

Lapithos drawings

An addition to the Cyprological collection of the Bank of Cyprus was made by the Scottish architect and painter, Christopher Connell. Twenty six drawings, made by him between 1970 - 71, when he was living in the now Turkish occupied area of Lapithos, have been kindly donated to the Foundation.

The drawings show houses, churches and, most importantly, scenes from everyday Lapithos life, such as Papa Timotheos, the priest; Phani Kakoulla, a woman working at the argalio and Charalambous Moyseos, pot maker.

CHAPTER 29

January 1987 we visited Ralph's stepmother, Lise, and her boyfriend, Joe, in Fuengirola, Spain. They lived in a nice apartment with an ocean view. They took us to Puerto Banus, a very picturesque little town. The ocean was full of luxury yachts. Ralph and I took a bus tour of Granada, Cordova, and Seville. It was all so beautiful, and the people were so friendly.

Ralph's mother was British. After several years she divorced her husband. She moved to Cyprus since she was also MI6. She lived on the army base at Episkopi, near Limassol. Ralph's father eventually married a lovely lady from Germany. Her name was Lise. Joe had been best friends with Ralph's dad. I believe he may have been Jewish; he was a well-known anthropologist. Anyway, after the death of Ralph's father, he and Lise became very close friends. They often visited us in Cyprus and attended our wedding. We were very fond of them both. They live in Fuengirola, on the coast, not too far from Barcelona.

CHAPTER 30

Now it turned out that Marilyn had been searching for her father for some fifteen years. She'd written letters to the Salvation Army to no avail, then to Somerset House in the UK, but she listed Rusty's birthdate the American way - month first, not realizing that in the UK the day comes first. She actually visited a seer with no luck, her pocketbook fifty dollars lighter. She attended tri-adoption league meetings and checked telephone directories from all over the world. All the information she had gathered was stolen from her car. When I was in London, en route to Cyprus, I contacted Salvation Army with all the details. Would you believe it - they finally found him living in Texas. After phone calls back and forth, Marilyn and her dad finally made contact after twenty-one years!

Custom Window Shades, draperies, bedspreads & accessories • lamp shades & a variety of window coverings. Complete Design Service 3295 Laguna Canyon Rd. Laguna Beach, CA 92651 714 - 494-7771

Our Business card

Marilyn

Taking a break

He flew to California to visit and met his two-year-old grandson for the first time. He informed them that he had re-married and divorced and that he had a daughter who was now Marilyn's half sister! They eventually met and became great friends. I met her mother, and we also became friends. Rusty was visiting California with his ex-wife and her girlfriend. I was in California helping Marilyn and Louise ready the shop for sale. Rusty was arriving with his female entourage to take Marilyn to lunch. I was supposed to disappear, but I refused. After all, this man had deserted us both some twenty years ago. I wanted to know if he had anything to say for himself.

The three girls went off to lunch. Rusty, after some small talk and obvious hesitation, finally asked me to lunch. He didn't eat much but enjoyed a couple of drinks. He finally made a statement that he had let me down and never tried to keep in touch with Marilyn. After all the time that had passed I no longer cared to hear his feeble statements. I didn't even feel like making any accusations. I never saw him again, thank God.

Rusty apparently lived alone with thirteen stray cats. He drank very heavily, mostly vodka, I believe. He died alone. Marilyn and her half sister, Tracy, flew to Texas to attend the funeral. I believe his alcohol intake over many years was the reason for his death.

CHAPTER 31

When I returned home to Cyprus, Ralph never even asked me for my decision; instead, he had gone ahead and made plans for our wedding. He had arranged to pay for our Welsh preacher and his wife to fly to Paphos and offered them a two-week holiday in a local hotel. He had talked to the owners of the beautiful Cypria Maris Hotel regarding holding our reception there. He'd discussed with our friend Jenny Adamos the possibility of her daughter, Natalie, being our bridesmaid. Also, as Jenny owned our favorite restaurant, Hondros, she agreed to make the wedding cake! I found myself going along with all these plans. He was so excited – what could I say?

In the end he paid for my brother to fly from South Africa to give me away. He paid for Marilyn and her three-year-old son Nicholas to fly from California. Nick would be ring bearer. He paid for Eric and his girlfriend to fly from California. Steven couldn't make it; he'd just started a new job. All the plans were made. Invitations were sent out to many of our Cypriot neighbors and friends, as well as to a few of Ralph's ex-girlfriends. We had a lovely wedding, first at the district commissioner's office and then at the beautiful and ancient St. Paul's Church. Our Welsh preacher presided, and later in the evening we had our reception. I got to wear three different outfits: one at the district commissioner's office, one at the church, and one at the reception.

The following day Eric and his girlfriend had to return to California. My brother had to return to South Africa. Ralph's best man, Michael Bichara, and his French wife joined us for a trip to the Troodos Mountains, as did Marilyn and Nicholas. Michael Bichara and Ralph had met and become friends while in Egypt. Michael was a Coptic Egyptian. The Coptics were Christians.

The hotel had organized a bucket of ice with champagne in our bedroom. After dinner I went up to the room to change into a sexy nightgown. I waited and waited and waited for Ralph to join me. He was still in the dining room, drinking wine and chatting. This was our honeymoon night!! I was furious by the time he showed up. I shouted at him, and he fell onto the bed. I shoved a pillow over his face. I wanted to kill him. Lucky for him there was a knock on our door; it was Marilyn. They were in the next room and could hear me shouting, so she was worried. She probably saved Ralph's life!

St. Paul's, centuries old. Our Wedding Church

The district commissioner married us first

My brother Mike (in dark glasses below) walked me down the aisle

Michael Bichara (behind Ralph his best man)

Then the Welsh minister married us

Wedding guests

Young love!

Welsh minister with ring bearer (my grandson Nicholas)
and bridesmaid Natalie (Andy's daughter)

Marilyn

Andy Adamos (white jacket) famous artist, father of our bridesmaid

Pamela's son Eric with girlfriend Rachelle

Reception at the Cypria Maris Hotel

Fozzie Bear dressed up. The waiter gives them an odd look!

Jenny made our cake

CHAPTER 32

When we returned to Paphos, it was obvious that Ralph's health was faltering. He'd been a heavy smoker for many years; eventually he quit, but he was now chewing Nicorette incessantly. He'd developed the unpleasant habit of trying to belittle me, especially after a few glasses of wine topped off with a neat whiskey. He'd sit at the kitchen table while I cooked lunch or washed dishes and make unpleasant remarks, perhaps out of boredom, or maybe provocation? It was very upsetting.

In desperation, I called our preacher and made an appointment to talk things over with him. He was very sympathetic; we discussed the problems for a while, after which he suggested that every time Ralph tried to intimidate me, I should just respond, "I know, but God loves me." I managed this advice for three days. Then, I'm ashamed to say, I erupted. I rushed over to where he was seated and tried to hit him on his head, but he held my hands away, so I resorted to kicking his shins until they were bleeding. Then I ran outside, took some deep breaths, and finally stopped shaking. In retrospect, I guess I should have disappeared whenever he started nagging at me. That would have been difficult when I was trying to prepare lunch.

A few days later we were visiting friends. Ralph pulled up his trouser leg to show them the wounds that I had inflicted. Their comment was, "I bet you bloody well deserved it!" They had known him for years.

The heavy intake of alcohol worsened. Now we were in separate bedrooms. His asthma also worsened so that he had to be on oxygen twenty-four hours a day. He would fall occasionally, but I wasn't strong enough to help him up. He was a big man with big bones. I would have to run across the street and ask our Cypriot gentleman neighbor to help.

Why? I asked myself why I had chosen three big drinkers to marry. Maybe it was because I had grown up with drinkers all around me. I found out that the few men I met who didn't imbibe were extremely boring.

CHAPTER 33

It was heartbreaking, but I decided to leave Ralph. He had been so good to me in many ways. He was always making sure that I never went too long without seeing my children, and he loved buying me a few beautiful outfits whenever he travelled alone. He was generous to a fault. When I told him I was going to return to the States, he said "Well, don't expect to hear from me. I won't be writing or calling you."

My daughter and son-in-law invited me to stay with them in Washington until I could decide what to do, where to go. They had a good-sized motor home in their backyard, which was just perfect for me. The day after I arrived, Ralph called! He said he missed me. He said he was planning to go to London to meet with his doctor. He wrote me long love letters. When he returned to Paphos, he called to tell me the doctor had said, "No more drinking or you'll die." So now he was begging me to come back to him. He'd completely stopped and would never drink again.

In a way, I still loved him, so, of course, I returned. We were married in March 1988 but together on and off since 1984. He was now a different person – quieter, not so boisterous, and fun-loving. It was difficult to get used to.

While I was in Washington, my ex-husband called me asking if I would come and stay for a couple of weeks to help him. Sadly, he had developed colon cancer, and he was very ill. Eric had been staying with him and caring for him after work, but he badly needed a break. I asked Ralph for advice before I returned to him. He said, "You must go to him; he is the father of your two sons, and he needs your help." Ed sent me a plane ticket, and I flew to California. Ed was very brave about his horrible illness. He continued to work some days; others, he didn't feel up to it. He had to wear a colostomy bag, which embarrassed him. In the evenings he'd have a beer and usually fall asleep right after dinner.

He took me to the airport for my flight back to Cyprus. I felt very sad saying good-bye. I knew I would never see him again. Two weeks later he called me to say he'd be waiting in heaven for me and reminded me to bring my tennis racquet! The boys told me later that he'd planned an exciting trip with them, but he passed away the night before. That was in January 1992.

Now I had returned to Cyprus and a very sober Ralph. He still chewed his Nicorette constantly. He stopped nagging me, which was a relief! He also stopped telling amusing stories and laughing loudly at them himself. His friends would say, "Ralph, for God's sake, have a drink." They wanted the old Ralph.

He grew very weak and sometimes stayed in bed all day. He made out his will. He lasted about two weeks after we took him to the hospital. The doctor took good care of him; he was a personal friend. Then one morning he called to say that Ralph had died. Good friends were staying with me, so they took me to the hospital. I laid a red rose on him. We stayed for a while. We sat by his bed and said a few prayers for him.

Ralph was gone. There was so much to do. His secretary helped me finalize his business affairs. We had to contact his business contacts in France, Oman, and United Arab Emirates. All of our belongings were sold or donated. We had three cats. Two were Siamese, Chang Mai and Pataya. Our big goofy black and white cat, Aspro, stayed with me when I moved in with a friend. Her daughter would look after Aspro. I left our car with a friend to sell. Friends helped me arrange Ralph's funeral. He did love Fozzie Bear, so we placed Fozzie in the coffin. It was now August 1994. We'd been together ten years. Many friends attended his funeral and came to join me in paying our last respects.

Ralph's funeral

CHAPTER 34

After a couple of weeks it was time to return to Washington. The motor home was sold, so now I had a nice, comfortable bed in the laundry room. The day after I arrived, the sadness of losing Ralph hit me. I literally went into deep mourning. I was also sad to have been parted from many close friends in Cyprus, as well as missing the island itself. I think I would have stayed, but I needed to be near my children and grandchildren. I was too depressed to leave my bed most days. The feeling was overwhelming. I couldn't imagine driving my car to town. It was difficult for Marilyn to imagine what I was going through. She was used to my being active and "alive."

It took a few weeks to finally climb out of my dark hole. I even started job hunting. I found one cleaning houses. It was low pay, but it got me up and out of the house. After a while, I applied to Sears for a career in what they called in-home decorating. The girl they employed was moving to another area of Washington, but she stayed on long enough to show me the ropes. After that, Sears sent me to Chicago to a huge nationwide training seminar.

I loved Chicago and found the training to be fairly easy as I had owned the Shady Ladies and had experience in various fabrics and home décor. We were treated well. There were comfortable accommodations and an enormous cafeteria with many choices of delicious food. I found a place to live – it was a mobile home in Suquamish – two bedrooms, lots of space, a decent-sized deck, and a small front garden, which I loved. My neighbors were American Indians, lovely people. The wife made me a very attractive necklace. I still wear it occasionally.

I had no lawn mower, so one sunny day I was lying down cutting the grass with a pair of scissors. It was a small lawn. Suddenly, a young man appeared. He was laughing at me! He left and returned with a lawn mower and insisted on mowing the lawn for me. Nice neighbors.

After two years working at Sears, Eric called me and suggested I return to California. He would fly to Washington. We'd pack as much as possible in my Volkswagen Rabbit, including my cat, Smokey. The rest of my belongings and furniture would be shipped. Sears very kindly agreed to transfer me to their branch in Laguna Hills, and I gave notice to my landlords. On the road again! I must say I was relieved to say goodbye to rain and sometimes snow and looked forward to the California sunshine.

Shortly after Marilyn and I had last visited South Africa, we were so sad to see that my brother was now in a nursing home. His lovely wife Helen took us to visit him every day, and the day before we left I told him, "*Mimi na penda wewe sana.*" That is Swahili for "I love you very much."

Mike said, "*Mimi na penda wewe zaidi.*" That meant, "I love you even more." Those were his last word to me. How I would miss him! He died two weeks later. He was always so entertaining, telling jokes and amusing stories. He had a special gift for accents; he could do Italian, French, German, South African, and Hispanic. We all miss his charisma, his love of nature, and his enthusiasm for life. I pray to see him again.

Before, when he was feeling well, we drove to a small game park for a picnic. When Mike got out of the car I quietly mentioned his fly was undone. He said, "Do not vorry, zee dead bird does not fall out of zee nest," in a French accent, of course.

As much as Mike and his wife loved Kenya, so much had changed since independence. So Mike upped stakes and took Helen and their small daughter Diana to Australia. But after a few months they missed Africa and decided now to return, this time to Durban, South Africa. Since Apartheid was over, some peace finally existed. They settled in Pinetown, a suburb of Durban. Mike secured a good job with Mercedes Benz. Helen worked for an accounting firm. It wasn't too long before they welcomed a new baby, Sarah, into the family.

Mike and his lovely wife, Helen, plus little Diana in Hong Kong
(and in the local costumes) on their way back to Africa.

Within my soul, within my mind
There lies a place J cannot find
Home of my Heart. Land of my Birth.
Smoke coloured stone and Flame coloured earth.
Electric skies, shivering heat
Blood red clay beneath my feet

Excerpt from Michelle Frost's wonderful poem, "Homeland"

Once back in California I found a nice apartment in Laguna Beach. Eric and Steve helped me move in. I missed Kenya terribly and thought about it every day. I couldn't stop remembering the wide open spaces and the beautiful animals roaming free. To quote Winston Churchill after his visit there:

Mombasa is the starting point of one of the most romantic and most wonderful railways in the world… all day long the train runs upward and westward through broken and undulating ground clad and encumbered with super-abundant vegetation. Beautiful birds and butterflies fly from tree to tree and flower to flower. Deep rugged gorges, filled by streams in flood, open out far below us through glades of palm and creeper covered trees. Every few miles are trim little stations, with their water tanks, signals, ticket offices and flower beds backed by impenetrable bush. In the evening a cooler, crisper air is blowing… at an altitude of four thousand feet we begin to laugh at the Equator… After the Makinda Station, the forest ceases, the traveler enters upon a region of grass… the plains are covered with wild animals.

So we admired the Africans. They had so little in the way of material possessions, but they were cheerful nonetheless. Sometimes, when we were young, we'd visit them in their grass thatched hats. They would invite us in to share the delicious stews they made with little rounds of *ugali* (maize meal). We'd press our thumbs into the rounds to make a dent and then used them to scoop up the stew.

I never returned to Kenya. I wanted to remember how it was when I left. Friends who did return for a visit advised me that it had changed drastically and that I would be disappointed. But still, away from the cities and small towns, there still existed beautiful countryside where you could feel safe. Safari camps exist for photographic tours…if you can afford them.

1959 beach in Durban

These guys wanted to be white!

A topless beauty with her chief

Mike and I in South Africa

Kenya

Some African animals

Some African animals

Some African animals

Some African animals

This notice was in a posh hotel in Durban

In retrospect, I now realize that my mother may have been Bi Polar. (Never heard of in those days. No therapy for anyone with mental problems—in Africa). She suffered mood swings. She was abusive towards me and even more so to my dad. For some reason, my brother seemed to evade most of her "down moods."

Between my mother's abuse and also some from the Convent Nuns, plus the horrific rape, I seemed strangely enough to build up some kind of inner strength.

Although there were times when I allowed other to make decisions for me.

I htnk my lucky stars that I've led such an interesting life with worldly travels and so many close friends.

I have three wonderful children, seven grandchildren, and one great granddaughter.

Now living in a 72 unit in San Clemente, California, for low-income seniors. All nationalities and personalities! Maybe they'll go into my next book.

The End